Best wishes to a g[...] person from
Dr. Ruth
and

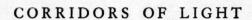

CORRIDORS OF LIGHT

Corridors
of Light

ELEANOR G. BROWN, Ph. D.

THE ANTIOCH PRESS • YELLOW SPRINGS, OHIO

Printed in The United States of America
by The Antioch Press, Yellow Springs, Ohio

Dedicated to
Alma M. (Mrs. Hugo) Dalmar

Contents

Introduction

Corridors of Light is one of the most interesting and moving autobiographies I have ever read. Here is a gifted woman, blind from her early infancy, beset by unpromising circumstances and financial limitations, who lives a long and radiant life, rich in public service as a teacher, a lecturer and an author. The book is an intimate self-revelation. It carries the reader into the secret thoughts and the daily experiences of a totally blind person, who by her faith, courage and ability turns trouble into triumph. One does not so much read this book as live it, reproducing in vivid imagination the experiences of the writer. How it feels to grow up as a blind child, what it involves to be the blind teacher of a roomful of sighted children in a city high school, how a blind person achieves a Master of Arts degree and a Doctor of Philosophy degree from Columbia University, and what it means to have a Seeing-Eye dog as one's closest friend—such experiences become vividly real to the reader of this fascinating book.

The book is written with humility and candor. Dr. Brown does not try to cover up her discouragements or to minimize her struggles. Now in her seventy-second year she opens the door to a wealth of memories. And such is her character that the total effect of her life-story is exhilarating. The dark shadows are there but the light wins in the end. One closes the book feeling that he has actually seen faith move mountains.

HARRY EMERSON FOSDICK

It is my joy in life to find,
At every turning of the road,
The strong arms of a comrade kind
To help me onward with my load.
And since I have no gold to give
And love alone must make amends,
My only Prayer is while I live,
"God make me worthy of my friends."

CHAPTER ONE

Dulled Arrow

I have been told that on one of the buildings of the National Cash Register Company are inscribed these words: "We progress through change."

My course in life has ever been charted thus.

I was born near Dayton, Ohio, in an area now a part of the Huffman Dam site in the shadow of Wright Field. The town in which I was born no longer exists; it was razed to serve as a reservoir for the Miami Conservancy. If there ever was a record of my birth, it cannot be found; but in the family Bible someone wrote: "Eleanor Gertrude, born August 28, 1887."

My eyes were large and blue. When I was three days old, my mother said I watched the curtain blowing in the breeze. If this is true, I must have been eager to make use of the little sight granted me for such a short while. A few days later my mother noticed that my eyes were cloudy and sore.

When the doctor was consulted, he said matter-of-factly, "Baby's sore eyes. Use cold tea and breast milk."

Little did he know the anguish my mother was to suffer, and the handicap I must always endure when he made this simple diagnosis. My eyes grew steadily worse. When I was nine days old the doctor brought his son to examine my eyes.

"You had better send for Dr. Green from Dayton," his son advised.

When the doctor arrived, he put my head between his knees and dropped nitrate of silver into my eyes. Mamma said the medicine smoked like a chimney. While she held my hands and feet, I went into one spasm after another. The doctor was using silver nitrate to burn out the infection, but my mother always

3

believed that he burned out the sight. In spite of the potency of the medicine, the treatment had come too late.

"Your baby will never see," the doctor said gently.

I have heard my mother tell this story many times, and always she cried. I never saw her cry about anything else. One sorrow my mother was spared, however; she never learned that I need not have been blind. Had silver nitrate been put into my eyes at birth, I could have seen as other children, and her burden would have been lessened. No one, not even the blind themselves, can comprehend the anguish of a mother whose child must live forever in darkness.

I have in my possession a picture of myself which was taken when I was six months old. I was sitting in a high chair. My white dress was long, reaching almost to the floor. My cheeks were plump and rosy and I was smiling, but my eyes were closed. Even in pictures I could not escape the inevitable.

Contrary to general belief, however, a blind child is a happy child. He runs, plays, sings, climbs, skips, jumps, like other children. There may be exceptions; but they are the result, not of blindness, but of the way the child is handled by his parents. My early days were happy ones. I lived with my mother, my sister, and my grandfather, but Mother was too busy to spoil me by waiting on me, so I was encouraged to do things for myself. My grandpa taught me to dress myself even when I was still too young to reach back and button my clothes. "That's the kicksie curlie that kicked his ma in the fire," he would say each time I would put my dress on over my head. I never knew quite what he meant, but I liked to hear him say it, and would hasten to please him. My grandpa was Pennsylvania Dutch and many of his sayings lacked interpretation.

My mother showed surprisingly good judgment in helping me cope with my problem of blindness. To increase my independence she allowed me to go places by myself. To independence I added adventure, imitating other children by climbing trees and fences and sliding down cellar doors, much to my mother's distress. It was her distress that made me realize that I was somehow different. Blindness then seemed not a depriva-

4

tion, but an advantage. I was allowed to draw the tickets at the lottery. My sister always had to take me with her when I cried to go along. I was often in the company of grown-ups, singing German songs and speaking pieces my grandpa had taught me. Perhaps too frequently, I was the center of attraction.

One of the problems of a blind child is the fear of the unknown. Animals always gave me a sense of foreboding. Grandpa had four pigs and I kept asking to see them, but always when he was ready to put my hands on one of them, I drew back in fear. One day he laughed and told me he would let me "ride the pig to butcher." I stood and heard the pigs squealing as they caught them, and when Grandpa came to get me, I ran away. That night I felt the meat in the big stone jars. I was disappointed. I didn't think a pig looked like that.

I used to walk along the street as close to the buildings as possible whenever a horse stood in the gutter. I could figure out the shadow between his front and hind legs, and his great head. When he whinnied and kicked the pavement, I was afraid of being trampled under his feet. Blind children should be allowed to touch as many animals as possible before they know fear. Every different animal presented a new problem to me, so until I had touched each one I still possessed a fear of it. No one had thought to put my hand on a dog when I was a baby, so I was four before I knew what a dog was like. The introduction was unexpected but pleasant when one day I accidently touched the silky ear of a neighbor's pet. From then on, all dogs were my friends.

That same year we moved into the big house on Main Street. Life for me there was full. I knew and talked with everyone in town, for Grandfather kept a restaurant just across from the hotel and depot. Our house was a three story structure with the restaurant in front and the living quarters opening on the side street. The most intriguing feature was the outside stairway opening into the back yard. At the foot of the stairs I had an imaginary organ with the music book on the step above. My mother thought I would be a musician because Blind Tom was. I never met Blind Tom and mother's prediction went amiss. Sometimes my organ became a table where I kneaded the pie dough which my mother baked and Grandpa ate, dirt and all. He knew better than to just pretend eating; my ears were sharp enough to detect any false sounds. I listened to him munching the brown crust and thought that he liked my pies better than my mother's.

The room in the house I loved best was the big sunny kitchen where each day Mamma baked thirty or forty large pies for Grandpa's restaurant.

"Eleanor," she would say as she stood beside the table rolling out pie dough and giving it little finishing pats with the rolling pin, "if I had a penny for every pie I've baked, we'd be rich, and I wouldn't have to worry about what will become of us."

There was an odor of apples cooking, of crust browning, of mince meat, and of grape juice burning. The kitchen was warm and friendly, and I wondered why my mother had anything to worry about. Sometimes as she kneaded the pie dough, she sang. In her gayer moods I remember her singing "Can she bake a cherry pie, Billy Boy, Billy Boy . . ." When she was sad, she sang such songs as "The Wind That Blows 'Crost the Wild Moor."

By the time I was four years old we seemed to have established quite a companionship. We sewed together, made beds, and did many simple household duties. No doubt I was in the way much of the time, and yet she never let me feel this. I know that I was ever my mother's first care, and though there seems to have been little outward affection between us, I realized that she loved me dearly. My affliction must have deepened Mother's feeling for me.

Sometimes my play took me into the back yard. One day, Mr. Schwartz, our butter and egg man, brought me a blind baby chick. He was prompted, I suppose, by our kindred deprivation. I watched the chicken's wing feathers grow and heard it fly down from the fence, but never heard it fly up. I guess it knew that in flying down, it would eventually hit the ground, but in flying up, it might not find the landing place. One night I put it to bed in its coal bucket with a piece of flannel tucked around it. The next morning it was dead. *Its* problems were over. My sister

6

wrapped it in silk and lace, but I refused to touch it.

Often the backyard grew too small for me. Sometimes I managed to get out, although usually my mother called, "Stay in the yard!" just in time to restrain me. On one such day I climbed the back fence. I placed my feet carefully on the lower girder, pulled myself up by the upper, and then held on to the top of the fence with one hand. Suddenly I became aware that something was in front of me. It must be a bird, I thought. Only birds are in the air. I drew back fearfully; then I noticed that the object, whatever it was, did not move, so I leaned my face closer. I could hear the rustling of leaves on the outside of the fence. It must be one of Mamma's sunflowers. Cautiously I extended my free hand. I was not afraid of flowers. My hand touched the largest sunflower I had ever seen. I liked the feel of its big yellow face with the brown eye, but its back felt ugly and rough. I wanted to keep it, but it grew outside the fence. In the evening when my mother was not around I pulled up the stalk and hid it. The next morning it was still in the yard but its petals were soft and old. It was mine, but I had robbed it of its glory, and I was sad and ashamed.

It should be remembered that blind people do not change their language because they do not see. So I may say, "I saw the flower," but mean "I felt the flower." This practice helps me maintain the normal means of communication. I could, however, just see color by holding the object close to the corner of my left eye. We used to have candy kisses wrapped in different colored papers. My grandfather would test me and because I held the paper so close to my nose in order to see it, the idea got around that I smelled the color. In the same way some believe that blind people tell color by touch. No sightless person I have ever known has been able to do this.

I was my grandfather's idol. I often used to wish that some of the affection he bestowed on me could have been given instead to my mother. He spent a great deal of time with me and many of my childhood memories include him. It was he who taught me how to tell money.

"A nickle is larger than a penny," he said, "and both have

7

smooth edges. A dime is smaller than a penny and has a rough edge. Quarters and fifty cent pieces are alike except for size."

Later, when I had paper money, I discovered I could not distinguish one bill from another, so I followed the practice of folding the various denominations in different ways.

In Grandpa's restaurant I turned the ice cream freezer and roasted the peanuts. As I turned the roaster I listened to the peanuts dancing like so many little wooden men. Sometimes my enthusiasm waned and Grandpa would talk of his imaginary little girl, Bessie, who lived in the cellar wrapped in his old coat. Grandpa said that if I wouldn't work, Bessie would. Once I insisted on seeing Bessie, so he let me feel his old coat and I believed she was inside.

One day Grandpa sang me a little song about McGinty.

> "Down went McGinty to the bottom of the sea,
> He must be very wet for they haven't found him yet,
> Dressed in his best suit of clothes."

Of course I wanted to know who McGinty was. The next day Grandpa brought me a little bottle. He said McGinty was inside. I shook the bottle and tried in every way to find McGinty, but with no success. Finally I broke the bottle, and sure enough inside was a little wooden man. My mother scolded me for breaking it, but how else was I to find McGinty?

Little did I dream then that there would be many things that I could not understand because I could not touch them. Once Grandpa and I went to a photographer to have our picture taken. The man lived in a house on wheels and traveled from town to town making tintypes. Before snapping the picture the photographer told me to "look at the birdie." I waited for him to put it into my hands and I didn't understand why he didn't show it to me. From this small beginning at the photographer's I grew to know that there would be many things which would come alive only in my imagination.

Often my imagination must have worked overtime. On Children's Day when I was four, my mother went with me to Sunday School. There were canaries in the windows. While the

8

minister was praying, the birds sang with all their might. Heaven must be like that, I thought. Back in the corner someone kept saying, "Amen." I believed it was God. I wished to be near Him and to touch Him.

My fertile imagination again displayed itself when my mother took me to the barber to have my hair cut for the first time.

"Mr. Jones," I said, "I want my hair cut red, short, and curly."

I really believed that Mr. Jones could carry out my orders. I got my hair brown, short, and wavy.

At no time was I allowed to cross the street alone, and many were the switchings I received for going to call on the blacksmith or the ticket agent.

"Oh, Mamma, I'll never run off again," I would wail.

I really thought I wouldn't, but in five minutes I had forgotten. Apparently I did not receive enough tannings, for the wanderlust is still strong within me.

I was also forbidden to cross the road that ran behind our house. Along this road the farmers drove their wagons and cattle, and once in a while a threshing machine rumbled slowly along. I have always feared large engines. They seem like huge monsters coming to mow me down. Fascinated, but afraid, I watched the threshing machine approach. I wanted to run away, but I stood flattened against the fence until it passed. I could not move because I could not hear where I was going.

However, Mother allowed me to go along Main Street, to the butcher's for weiners or to the grocer's for a candy doll in which I might find a prize penny, or a candy sheep with a bell on it. All of the stores were on our side of the street with an occasional alley separating them. Part of the sidewalk was cement and part was boards. The alleys, the boards, and the cement aided me in locating the various stores.

One day in the spring before I was five, Mamma sent me to the bakery for bread. To my confusion I dropped the dime she had given me in the crack of the board walk. I went home in tears and was given another which I also lost. Still my mother did not scold me but urged me to stop crying so that Grandpa would not know. The next day I dropped a stack of saucers I was drying, and my mother remarked to my sister how nervous I was. The third day a blood vessel burst in my left eye and Dr. Marquardt was called. Two years earlier I had had brain and spinal fever, and now another illness had begun.

Realizing that my illness was to be a long one, Mamma had my bed moved downstairs into the front room. In this room I had poked my fingers through the isinglass in the stove, had examined the red plush album with the big gold clasp and had felt the photographs inside and tried vainly to guess whose they were. In the corner of the room was a whatnot where Mamma kept her choicest possessions. Only on rare occasions was I permitted to examine these treasures. Outside on the doorstep I had counted the slats on the shutter, had said "rich man, poor man" as far as my hands could reach. On the same steps I had stamped my feet and yelled and listened to someone answering me. The echo for me may have held the same charm that the shadow holds for the child who can see. I thought of all this now as I lay in bed.

"St. Vitus Dance," the doctor called my ailment. Finally the twitching ceased and I became paralyzed.

"Edna, it will be a higher power than mine that can save her," Dr. Marquardt said.

My mother made no sound. I begged that if I were going to die, I wanted to be dressed in white so that I would be ready.

Dr. Marquardt used an electric battery on my back for the paralysis.

"This treatment is strong enough for three men," he explained, but still I did not feel it.

When the sponge finally tickled me, my mother cried for joy, and the doctor carried me jubilantly around the room.

Twice I had St. Vitus Dance and twice I was paralyzed all over, and yet the complete use of my body was restored to me.

When I recovered, Dr. Marquardt told my mother that I probably would not live long. I was learning my sister's lessons and though I was just five, he suggested that I be sent to school in order that I might glean all I could while I was still able.

"Superintendent Burrows, an old classmate of mine, is head of the State School for Blind in Columbus," Dr. Marquardt said. "That will be an excellent place to send her."

Dr. Marquardt was a country doctor, but he possessed a philosophy of life which gave me my chance, and he has always inspired me.

As soon as the doctor suggested it, preparations for my going to school began.

"Eleanor," my mother said, trying in some way to make me understand the problem, "when you go to school, you will be gone for a long time. You won't come home for dinner or supper or at night. You won't see Grandpa or Katherine or any of us for months."

"How long is months?" I asked, undaunted.

"It's so long, I can't tell you how long," my mother answered.

"But I want to go to school. I want to learn to read like Katherine, and to spell."

"You're going to get to go," my mother continued, "but you can't cry to come home. If you go, you must stay a long time."

Still I wanted to go. My mother did not tell me why I could not come home when my sister could and somehow I did not ask. My mother always refrained from speaking of my blindness and so perhaps there grew up between us a kind of barrier. Many of the things which I might have discussed with her were not mentioned because of the reticence which existed between us.

I had never spent a night away from my mother, so she planned that I should visit with Annie Fisher, a friend of the family. Annie had two younger brothers, and all afternoon and evening they played with me and entertained me. It was always harder for me to play by myself when I was not at home. I was on unfamiliar ground, and I felt shy and ill at ease. As evening came, I grew more quiet. I thought of my sister doing the dishes, of my mother sewing and singing, of Grandpa in the store giving me a piece of candy. The boys continued to play with me until bedtime. I was going to sleep with Annie. I was slow about taking off my clothes so Annie undressed me and tumbled me into bed. I heard her comb her hair, open and close the drawers, and take off her shoes.

"Out goes the light," she said, and as soon as she said it, I knew it was now or never.

"I want my Mamma," I said without crying.

Annie did not try to dissuade me. She simply helped me to dress and took me home. I can still remember my return. My mother had pulled the sewing machine next to the table and Annie sat me on the table and told my mother just what had happened. I could hear the lamp singing beside me. Mamma seemed glad to see me and I was so glad to get home. When Annie was gone, my mother reminded me, "When you go to school, you can't come home at night."

"But I want to go to school," I protested.

"And leave me?" my mother questioned.

"I want to go to school and I won't cry." And I never did cry, until I was in my teens.

So the preparations went forward. My mother used every spare minute to sew. Sometimes she stood me on a chair to fit me. It was hard to stand still and always I had the feeling that I might fall. My mother made all of my clothes. I remember there were nine aprons, two for Sunday and the rest for everyday. My aprons were gathered full into narrow yokes with deep ruffles around the neck and arms. The "telescope" was brought down from the attic. This old fashioned case was made of two rectangular parts, one of which fitted into the other and was held together by straps and a handle. I sat on it beside my mother as she sewed. When the "telescope" was packed, it was almost twice as high as it had been before. My mother was going to make sure that I had enough clothes to keep me clean while I was away.

When the day came for me to start, Mamma dressed me, for I was too excited and happy to do it myself. I was going to school, and all these pretty new clothes were mine. There were my shoes with patent leather tips, buttons, and a red tassel; my starched petticoat, so stiff it stood alone; my blue luster dress Empire style, trimmed with yellow silk and gold braid; my blue bonnet and coat edged with white fur. I had never felt so dressed up before. My hair was curled around my face, my cheeks were glowing, my lips were smiling. But my large blue eyes were sightless.

On the train I tried to visualize what the School for Blind at Columbus would be like. It must be, I thought, like the Lutheran Church: There would be a long flight of steps leading up to the front door; inside would be rows and rows of benches. It wasn't like that at all. It was much more wonderful. It was more wonderful than anything I have ever seen or imagined.

CHAPTER TWO

Bittersweet

I sat in a big chair in the office listening aimlessly to my mother and Superintendent Burrows. I kept swinging my feet back and forth saying to myself, "When do I go, when do I go, when do I go to school?" Suddenly my hand discovered a decoration on the end of the chair arm. I was sure it was a face. There were two eyes, a big nose, an open mouth, and on either side of the teeth were long fangs.

"That's a lion's head, Eleanor," Dr. Burrows said as he noticed my perplexity. I wondered if it was put there for little girls like me to see.

"She's rather young and small for our school," Superintendent Burrows was saying.

"I think I would not mind so much if Eleanor were a little older," my mother said, "but the doctor thinks it's best, and she wants to come."

"That's half the battle," Dr. Burrows commented.

"I want to go to school," I interrupted. "I want to learn to read and spell like Katherine."

Miss Perry, the little girls' matron, hurried in. She was large, capable, and kind.

"So here's our new baby," she said, lifting me out of my chair. "That's a big chair for such a little girl."

The superintendent had finished writing and talking, so Miss Perry took my mother and me down the corridor to the right and up four flights of steps. There were no elevators in those days.

"The little girls live on the third floor," Miss Perry said. "The dining room and the classrooms are on the first floor and the

14

chapel is on the second."

Miss Perry took us to her room first. As soon as we were seated, she sent for Katie.

"Katie was our youngest child; now Eleanor will be the baby," she said. In a few minutes Katie came across the wooden platform that led into the matron's room.

"Katie, we have a new playmate for you," Miss Perry said.

"Hello! What's your name?" Katie asked as she stood beside me. Then with quick eager fingers she began examining me from head to foot. I wasn't used to this. I felt pictures and books and toys when I was by myself or with my mother, but I didn't examine people. Katie, however, knew all about me in those first few minutes. Both of us were trying to interpret the world through the sense of touch, but I was shy and Katie was less restrained.

"What color is your dress?" Katie asked. I noticed that her voice was deep and husky and she had a slight lisp.

"Blue," I said proudly.

"Do you like going to school?" my mother asked Katie.

"Yes, ma'am."

"Do you get homesick for your mother?"

"Not very often."

"I want to go to school," I chimed in, "and I won't cry."

Miss Perry took us to the room where I was to sleep. Katie went along.

"Your room is number eight," Miss Perry said. "We call it the baby room. The youngest girls sleep here."

Suddenly a loud bell began to ring. "There's the dinner bell," Katie said, taking my hand. She and I ran downstairs together and my mother and Miss Perry followed.

"Aren't you going to say good-bye to me?" Mama asked, as I hurried into the dining room. I kissed her quickly and went with Katie.

There were three hundred boys and girls in that dining room. Everybody talked at once and I thought I had never heard so much noise. Someone tapped a bell and the room grew very still. Then we sang: "Dear Father above, to Thee we offer

15

Thanks. Bless Thou our hearts and help us all each day to do Thy will. Amen."

We sat at large horseshoe-shaped tables and the waitress served us from the inside. In the afternoon, because it was New Year's, there was a social. At that social I was questioned and examined by boys and girls alike. Many times in the years to come I would be in the group who would participiate in this ceremony.

"What's your name, little girl?"

"How old are you?"

"Where do you live?"

"How much can you see?"

"Have you ever been to school before?"

And as I answered the many questions hurled at me, eager fingers examined my hair, dress, and height while other children stood by and listened.

Priscilla was a friend of Miss Perry. "When do we go to school?" I asked Priscilla after I had been examined and re-examined.

"New Year's is a holiday," Priscilla told me. "School begins tomorrow."

The next morning as soon as I heard the sound of the rising bell I jumped up and dressed. Miss Perry came over to help me, but she was surprised to find that all I needed was buttoning. One of the girls in the baby room was eleven, but she was still there because she had never been taught by her parents to put on her clothes. As she grew older she became more sensitive and the tasks she was supposed to perform became more difficult. So it is that the longer we postpone doing simple things the more arduous is the undertaking. The kindest thing you can do for a blind person is to teach him to help himself.

After breakfast when the bell rang again, everybody went to chapel. The girls formed a double line on one side of the center and the boys on the other. Katie and I led the line and I felt grown-up and important as I marched in in time with the organ and piano. The little girls sat down in front. First we sang, "Master, the Tempest Is Raging." I had never heard that song

16

before. Singing made me feel a little homesick inside. I wondered why they kept singing, "Geese, be still." How could I know they were singing, "Peace, be still"? Then Dr. Burrows read the Bible and prayed. During the prayer Mamie, one of the other little girls, cried, "I want my mamma!" I thought of mine, but I was proud not to be homesick.

After Dr. Burrows had given us a resumé of the daily news, Katie took me to the first grade class. In the school room there were desks on either side. I was too small to sit at the desks so I was placed in a kindergarten chair beside Miss Cook, the teacher. When I sat down my hand touched her dress. It was luster like mine. To me she was a being wonderful beyond compare for I thought she knew all I wanted to learn. Her skin, when I touched her hand, was smooth like the petal of a rose and there was a fragrance of roses about her.

The first hour was arithmetic. I had learned to count to a hundred and now we were learning the multiplication tables. We sang them to help us to remember and I joined in because I liked to sing. I soon discovered that blind people do all their arithmetic, algebra, and geometry mentally; working a problem by adding or subtracting our columns from the left while other people work from the right. If I want to add one hundred and sixty-five and two hundred and forty-three, I add my hundreds first, which gives me three hundred; sixty and forty make another hundred, which makes four hundred; and five and three are eight. So the answer to the problem is four hundred and eight. It sounds complicated, though it is simple for a blind person.

While we were singing our multiplication tables, someone came and took me to the reception room. There was my mother. She seemed glad to see me, but I hated to leave the arithmetic class.

"I must go, Mama," I said as the bell began to ring.

"Aren't you going to stay a little while?" my mother asked. She was crying, but I didn't stay. I hurried back to the first grade room eager to continue the lessons.

Spelling came next. The first grade was far ahead of me, so I listened to them spell *ring*, *sing*, *bring*, *fling*, and *sting*, and I

17

contributed my bit by spelling *dog, rat, cat, sat,* and *hat.* Our spelling had to be committed to memory and the words were given over and over again so that everyone would learn them. Blind children are apt to be poor spellers unless they spend a great deal of time memorizing the words. Sometimes I say to myself, "Is there one *t* in petal or two?" First I think it is one way and then the other. And finally I can't be sure. I can not, as a sighted person does, jot down the word to see if it looks right. Blind children have no visual images of words. The study of languages has improved my spelling.

Blind children need to learn how to play and use their hands and often we formed a circle, putting our toes on tacks driven into the floor; then we sang, "Good morning, Merry Sunshine" and "Daffy-Down Dilly." We played a flower game with balls covered with different colored yarn. There was red for the poppies, yellow for the tulips, and blue for the flags. I was given a tulip, and when they sang about it, I stepped to the center of the circle and held it up. Later, we sat at low tables and pasted chains of different colored links together, stuck pegs in boards, wove paper mats, strung wooden beads, and made clay birds' nests.

Miss Cook brought an owl from the stuffed animal case. We were all supposed to examine it so we would know how an owl looked, but I did not do much investigating, for I was afraid.

In the afternoon I went to Fancy Work. I was given a metal tray with three compartments containing different colors of beads. My task was to learn to fish them onto a wire and when I could fish them rapidly and count what I gathered, I would be ready to make a bead basket. This kind of work is not practical, but it does help blind children to learn to use their hands.

It was my reading lessons, however, that I remember most vividly. I was seated at a kindergarten table. Miss Cook gave me a chart. It wasn't anything like my sister's school books. There were two alphabets on the chart, one in dots, and one in raised letters like those on Mason jars. Miss Cook said the dots were called New York Point and the others were Line Print. She showed me "a" in both systems, and told me to look at the letters until I was sure I would know them whenever I saw them.

When she began working with the other children I buried my head in my arms and sat for a long time. I had been troubled before but never like this.

"Are you sleepy?" Miss Cook asked. "It's pretty early for a little girl to get up."

"I'm not sleepy."

"You aren't homesick?" she laughed.

"No, ma'am. I want to learn to read like Katherine."

"You are going to read like Katherine," Miss Cook said kindly.

"Katherine holds her book in her hand and looks at it, but I feel the letters with my finger."

"The Line Print looks like your sister's book," Miss Cook suggested, "but when you can't see you learn to read with your fingers. It's ever so much nicer than not being able to read at all."

A single tear escaped and rolled down my cheek.

"You don't want the class to think you're homesick, do you?" Miss Cook asked.

"I'm not homesick."

Reluctantly I began examining my chart again, not pacified but accepting the inevitable, and the inevitable was bittersweet. I had believed that by going to school I would be able to read the printed page. Though I was only five I knew now this would never happen.

With play and work my first school day ended. That night when I said my prayers I meant to say, "Please, God, make me learn to read like Katherine." But I said only, "Please, God, make me learn to read." That day I lit the first of many candles for my darkness.

CHAPTER THREE

Castle of Light

After my first day in school, I remained only two months. Another illness similar to the last forced my mother to take me home. When I recovered, I was almost six. During my illness I did not know that my grandfather had decided to break up housekeeping, so I was surprised on coming down stairs for the first time to find tables everywhere loaded with all kinds of crockery and dishes.

"We're getting ready for an auction," my mother said.

"What's an auction?" I asked.

"It means selling all of our belongings," my mother explained, "and then we're going to live someplace else."

"Where are we going to live?" I asked.

"I don't know yet," my mother said abruptly, "but in a few months you will go back to school and Katherine and I will go to work."

"Who is going to cook for Grandpa?" I inquired.

"Grandpa is going to have a little store across the railroad, and he will take care of himself." Grandpa was getting old, and since I would be in school he seemed no longer interested in keeping the family together.

My mother found a little house for the three of us, and there we spent the summer. Mamma tried to support my sister and me by taking in baking and sewing. One day a woman engaged her to make a black taffeta dress. Dress-making was not simple in those days; there were French seams to be made, whalebones to be sewed in, and dozens of hooks and eyes to attach. The garment had to be finished as perfectly inside as outside. When the woman came again, Mother had the dress finished. However, the woman was so pleased with it and talked so much about it, that she left

20

without paying my mother for her work.

Another event of that summer stands out vividly in my mind. The house in which we lived was built low to the ground and it was not difficult to climb onto our roof. One night I awoke to hear heavy footfalls overhead.

"Mamma," I cried, "there's someone on the roof!"

"You're dreaming," my mother suggested. The three of us lay there listening breathlessly. There it was again, the sound of someone walking on our roof. I cried miserably. I was still nervous from my illness, and was wretchedly afraid. Finally, Mother said, "It's probably Mr. Young, the landlord. He's afraid he won't get his rent, so he is walking on the roof to scare us and make us move."

"I want to go to Grandpa!" I cried. So my mother dressed me and took me to him. The next day when we went back to our little house we found foot prints on the roof, but there were no other traces of our mysterious visitor. I was afraid to stay, but my mother told me that she would take me back to school in a couple of days. Yet I wondered what would become of my mother and Katherine. It was a blessing that for nine months out of each year Mamma need not worry about me.

The School for Blind became for me not only a school, but a home; and my feeling for it has grown with the years. It has always been for me a wonderful place, so wonderful that description fails to convey the poetry and romance which I always associate with it. Gradually, as time passed, I began to think of is as a castle of light. It had brought me light in darkness; it had opened my mind, though it could not open my eyes.

The building was T-shaped, with wings at either side. The center shaft of the T separated the boys' and girls' dormitories.

The walls of the buildings were of rough grey stone and I suppose that is why I always thought of it as an enchanted castle. They were very thick and my roving fancy led me to imagine that within them wound secret staircases leading to dungeons beneath the cellar and to hidden tower rooms. These walls furnished a unique diversion. There were narrow, sloping ledges around the building, three and five feet from the ground.

The timid children walked around the three foot ledge holding to the rough notches in the stone. Those who were more bold climbed higher. At night when they were supposed to be asleep, some of the older boys used to walk in the eaves trough eighty feet above the ground. They were not troubled by the dizzy heights, and if they were afraid, they hid their fear with a show of bravado in order to impress the other students.

The halls were long and wide, and the floors were a checkerboard of black and white stones. I soon learned how to measure my steps so that I could play hopscotch on them.

Separating the center of the building and the other corridors were heavy iron doors which must have been placed there in case of fire. They were always kept open, and since there were two of them on either side of the hall, they could be folded so as to make snug playhouses.

Opening from the halls was a court which served as a playground. There were teeters there, and sometimes when I was particularly brave I walked up them and ran down. Often six or eight girls teetered on either end. There was a big iron swing which held a dozen children. The big girls stood up in front, pumping with their feet until the swing went up into the treetops and almost turned over. In the center of the court was a summer house built around a huge oak beneath which I liked to play. One day I heard a dull chopping and a sickening cracking and tearing.

"They are cutting down the old oak in the court," Miss Cook said, and I felt as though they were tearing out my heart. Where the courts had been, they built gymnasiums with glass roofs and smooth, slippery floors. I never liked the gymnasiums, because they seemed to me like interlopers.

The windows in the school were high and deep set, and their sills sloped down inside and out. Once Ada Mae, who was five, wanted to see how far down the ground was, so she jumped sixty feet. She caught on a bush, and her only injuries were a few scratches on her chin!

The stairways were long, consisting of about fifteen steps to a flight, and the banister that ran from the top of the stairway to the bottom was in the shape of a spiral. What a wonderful slide it would make, I thought, but I noticed with regret that from the first landing downward the banister was dotted with little inch-high obelisks to keep us from sliding. Rumor had it, however, that some of the boys used to start from the top and go all the way down to the first landing, jumping off before they reached the points.

In the fall when I was six my education began in earnest. I learned to read, spell, and count, but my lessons in writing New York Point had to wait until I was older. I was also taught to do bead work in order to learn to use my hands. But I liked reading best, and I spent most of my free time with my books. Even though I could not see to read like my sister Katherine, I was rapidly learning to use the resources at my disposal to make a whole new world come alive under my fingertips.

That first Christmas I did not go home. There was no money for my railroad fare. Besides, I had no home to which I could go. There was a Christmas tree in the kindergarten room where the window shutters were closed, and the only lights in the room were from the candles on the tree. I remember sniffing the odors of melting wax, pine, and oranges and hearing the sizzle of the candles. Then, suddenly, there was a sound of sleigh bells coming nearer and nearer. I was so excited I could hardly breathe.

"Merry Christmas, boys and girls," a voice boomed. It sounded just like the voice of Jerry, the man who met me at the station when I came to school. It was funny, I thought, that Santa Claus should talk like Jerry. But when he gave me dishes and a little cupboard, I knew it was Santa Claus for sure.

Christmas, too, was a time for boxes from home. For days we listened at the windows for the sound of the expressman's wagon and the muffled clop-clop of his horse's hoofs on the snowy road. Then there was a mad rush downstairs to the entrance of the dining room where the boxes were always placed. One of the girls who could see fairly well read the names. Eagerly I examined the contents of my boxes and distributed them among the girls and my favorite teachers.

The next summer I stayed with my grandfather. Grandpa was always lots of fun; he played with me and told me stories.

23

"There was once a woman," he said in his jolly way, "who never wanted to work. One day someone went through the street crying, 'Corn meal to give away, corn meal to give away.' 'Is it sifted?' the woman called. 'No,' the donor answered, 'Drive on in your cart,' the woman ordered!"

Later that summer I developed a bad case of whooping cough. My grandfather did not know how to care for me, so he sent for my mother, who was working in Dayton. I was glad to see her, but discovered that she had no place for me to live. The woman she worked for would not allow her to keep me. So I was taken to a home which was supported by some ladies of a church. My mother came to see me twice a week and brought me fruit, cakes, and sandwiches to eat. I used to gobble them up as fast as I could.

"Why don't you save them till I'm gone?" my mother suggested. "Then you will have something to do and won't get so lonesome." How could she know that I was too hungry to wait? At breakfast we were urged to eat our oatmeal without milk or sugar and our bread without butter in order to send the money thus saved to the "heathen." How I hated the "heathen."

Every evening we had prayers, and as the children stood and sang, "God Be With You Till We Meet Again," I cried for my mother. At night we slept three or four across a double bed, depending upon how many children were in the home.

For a time, however, there was one bright spot in this picture of misguided Christianity. A tiny baby was brought to the home; his name was Benny. He had been deserted. I loved Benny, and I spent most of my days wheeling him back and forth on the sidewalk or rocking him in the sewing room. One day I was not allowed to rock Benny, and the next day they told me he had died. I was lonely again.

When I became ill from lack of nourishment, my mother decided to take me out of the home. School would soon begin, and once more I would be cared for. Most of my clothes were missing, at least the matron could not find them. My blue bonnet with the white fur was gone, and my winter coat, too.

That fall I was glad to go back to school, even though it meant leaving my mother. The summer had made a lasting im-

24

pression on me; I was beginning to learn the misery of being without a home, and the trouble and heartache of blindness.

Back at school in the fall we gathered locust beans on the south lawn. As we handled them, the pods made a rustling sound like taffeta. The inside of the pod was filled with a sticky substance and a number of small beans, and when we had enough beans saved, we made a bean bag. The advantage of locust beans is that they never get shriveled and dry, and they are harmlessly light in weight. Sometimes we tried throwing them through a frame which we had previously located.

My mother sent me a jumping rope, but I never seemed to be able to turn it successfully when I jumped. Sometimes, however, we had a long rope and while two of the girls turned, Carrie and I would jump together. She could see a bit and could tell just when to start so that we would jump in unison.

I began to study geography in the third grade. The maps could be taken apart. The parts were fitted together like a jigsaw puzzle and each piece represented a state. The mountains were raised, the rivers cut in, the cities marked with tacks, and the ocean was smooth and lower than the land.

First we learned about the New England states. Then Miss Harding, our teacher, said, "Boys and girls, I want you to come in and study the map. Learn the boundaries and location of the states, and pay special attention to their shapes and size."

I was eager to see what the map looked like, so I returned to the third grade room after school. I could scarcely reach Maine, the map stood so high on its easel. When I took out Massachusetts, Rhode Island came too. When I tried to put these two back, out fell Connecticut and Vermont. Things grew steadily worse as the United States collapsed, state by state, on the floor around me. I couldn't get it back together again.

I worked at it after supper, and when the bell for evening chapel rang I still continued the Humpty-Dumpty puzzle. Finally, tired and discouraged, I went quietly to my room, hoping to avoid discovery. I should have waited until chapel was over and gone up with the other girls, but I was not clever at deception. I crept into bed, and the bed squeaked; it was wooden and old. Suddenly, before I could realize what had happened, I was on the floor. The bed, too, had fallen down. The crash brought Miss Avey, the new matron, who added a scolding to my misery; but finally when I told her my tale of woe, she laughed.

Still I wondered what Miss Harding would say. After hours of worry, I was surprised the next morning to find that she had put the states back and said nothing.

Miss Harding was one of us. She had attended the School for Blind, and now she was teaching and reading to us by means of a magnifying glass. She taught me to appreciate poetry. We all loved her and were proud when her brother became President of the United States.

At Christmas time Miss Harding chose two of us to learn "I Heard the Bells on Christmas Day." It was to be recited to music, and the one who did the better job was to give it in the chapel on Christmas Eve. Paula was three years older than I, but she didn't read well to music. I worked like a Trojan, and I knew I was doing better than she was. Two days before Christmas, Miss Harding sent for me. When I received her message, I was sure I was going to be selected. As I stood before her, Miss Harding said, "Eleanor, I shouldn't have had two of you learn that poem. You're doing better than Paula, but she is so unhappy about it that I think we should give it to her."

I agreed, though I wondered how she could think I would not mind. I had thrilled to the lines of the poem, and it had seemed to me that I would be giving the audience a message, a message of hope and justice. I was so disappointed at Miss Harding's decision that Christmas for me that year was spoiled. Yet I knew that she was asking of me the kind of sacrifice that she herself would have been glad to make. I was ashamed of my selfishness and disappointment.

Miss Judy was my fourth grade teacher. I remember her for two things. She was exceedingly religious, and she taught us many beautiful hymns. In her school room was an organ which she played for us whenever she was free.

I recall when Miss Judy persuaded me to be converted and give my heart to Jesus. As she played the organ we sang together

26

"Just As I am"; then Miss Judy read from the Bible about "Suffer the little children to come unto me." As she prayed for a long time, I bowed my head reverently on my hands. When she had finished she asked me to pray. I prayed, "Dear Jesus, help me to be a good Christian, and to learn my lessons every day."

Then we sang, "There Is Sunshine In My Soul," and when I went from her, I felt clean and free. It seemed to me that I was walking on air. I found myself singing the rest of the day, and I carry the memory of that spiritual uplift with me still.

I began my piano lessons when I was about nine. I did not start by learning the staff as most children do.

"Well, Eleanor," Miss Ernst said, "now you're going to learn to play the piano." It was almost as exciting as learning to read. Miss Ernst was blind, too.

"Just above the keyhole," she said, "is middle C."

Then she taught me the scale. When I was able to play the scale, she dictated my first finger exercises. I really had no musical ability, but I acquired a deep appreciation for music from which I still derive pleasure and comfort.

The school was not built with recreation rooms. Most of the time we played the old-fashioned games, "The Farmer-in-the-Dell" and "London Bridge," either in our bedrooms or in the corridors. However, when we tired of these, we made up games of our own. One I remember in particular was dubbed "Giant," and I believe I was the originator. I had always loved thrilling fairy tales of castles and giants. The "Giant" stayed in his castle between the two chests of drawers while everybody tried to get past him without being caught. Sometimes we went over and under the beds. The game was more difficult if the giant could see partially, and all of us tried to sneak past him if he were blind, although he usually heard us. The first time we were caught, it was a bite; the second time, we lost an arm; the third time we lost our heads and became "Giant." Sometimes the girls collided with one another, and if they didn't lose their heads in the process, they certainly damaged them!

At seven o'clock every weekday evening we went to reading. I especially remember the night Miss Tracy was reading *Tom*

Sawyer to us. I was particularly enamored of "Injun Joe." At nine o'clock we were supposed to be in bed, and at a quarter past nine the matron came, put out the lights, and saw that we were all tucked in safe and sound. But I couldn't forget "Injun Joe." Cautiously I crept from bed to bed, saying in a spooky voice, "Injun Joe, Injun Joe!" Sadie, suddenly awakened, screamed and I scrambled into bed as ominous footsteps approached along the corridor. Sadie's screams had brought the matron. I was sent to bed right after supper the next night.

When I was in the fifth grade, I began my sewing lessons. On Tuesday we darned the younger children's stockings, on Friday we practiced threading needles, and the rest of the week we made linens for the school. It should be remembered that when a blind child is being taught to make something, the work must remain in *his* hands, and the operation must be guided, not done by the teacher. Miss Benton was my first sewing instructor. She gave me a darner and showed me how to tie the stocking down over it. While we were working, Miss Benton read to us, for her own pleasure and our supposed edification, one of the dime novels of the day.

"Eleanor," Miss Benton would say, looking up from her reading, "over one, under one." I had forgotten about my darning as I drank in the romantic words of sentimental love.

Miss Benton was soon replaced by Mrs. Sheldon. When she came, the department took on a business-like atmosphere, and I began hemming towels, napkins, and sheets. After the sheets were basted, I was allowed to hem them on the sewing machine. The foot on the sewing machine was straight, not curved, and the left prong of the foot extended beyond the right. By keeping my finger on the left prong, I was able to make a straight seam or stitch a hem. I have never known a totally blind person to sew his finger. If the needle runs off the hem, it makes a different sound. I liked sewing on the machine. It was a quick way to get something done.

Threading a machine needle is easy. Bend a horse hair or wire into a loop, run the loop through the eye of the needle, then the thread through the loop; pull the loop back through the needle and the thread will come with it. On Friday we put away all of our sewing and sat threading needles, as many of them as we could, for an hour. I started with a darning needle and a piece of heavy thread. I twisted the end of the thread tightly between my fingers, put the head of the needle in my mouth, felt the eye with my tongue, then tried to poke the thread through. Beside me sat Bertha. She could thread a number twelve as quickly as I could manage a darning needle. I never got beyond a number seven, and that rarely. Nowadays when I sew, which is seldom, I use a self-threader needle; the eye has a spring in it which opens when the thread presses against it.

When I had made sheets and pillow cases until I thought the whole school must be overstocked, I was allowed to sew something for myself. I chose a petticoat. From the tissue paper pattern, I cut another of wrapping paper. When my brown paper pattern was completed, I pinned it in turn onto the cloth. Since I knew how to seam and hem and gather, the rest of the work was comparatively easy until I came to the buttonholes. I practiced on another piece of cloth until I could make at least a pig's eye. I am glad I do not have to make my own clothes, for if I did, I'm afraid I would not have many.

I was eleven when I began typewriting. Up to that time one of the teachers had always written my letters home. I learned the keyboard, using the touch system just as a sighted person does, and I practiced by writing over and over, "The quick brown fox jumps over the lazy dog." Since most people use the touch system, a blind person can type with equal efficiency. Soon I was writing to my mother, and I remember how proud she was of my first letter. Typing is a blessing to the blind, the only disadvantage, of course, being that they cannot read what they have written.

I always enjoyed writing compositions and I seemed to possess a tendency for creative writing. First, I would write a theme using the dot system. When I had made it as correct as I could, I copied it on the typewriter. The typewritten copy, however, always had to be checked by somebody who could see. The *Citizen*, a Columbus paper, offered a prize of two dollars for the best story written by a child under fourteen. I won the first prize for girls when I was twelve. The story was called "Tears Will Mingle With Joy" and it appeared in the paper along with my picture. I was radiantly happy and spent my two dollars at the park on popcorn, peanuts, and rides.

I tried my hand also at writing poetry, and though I still turn out doggerel, I have found pleasure in doing it and occasionally compose a stanza that is not too bad. We were encouraged to commit to memory as much poetry as possible.

In school we were taught to sing, first in kindergarten, then in junior choir, and later in senior choir. I was also given vocal lessons. The songs I liked I sang well from words and music written in Braille which had superseded New York Point. I learned them in my practice hours and then I went to my teacher and we worked them out with accompaniment. I held second place among the sopranos in the choir. I have visited a great many schools, but the young people of the School for Blind sing as well as any chorus I have ever heard. We always sang one hymn in chapel during the week, but on Sunday we sang two. After Sunday School, we went out into the city to church. As the time drew near for us to leave, everybody began inquiring about the weather. I used to pray for rain, and when it came and the order to remain at home was given, a shout of joy filled the corridor. For then we could read or sleep. Sunday was reserved as a day of quiet. When the weather was inclement, our amusement was walking up and down the corridor singing songs and hymns.

From year to year, we learned to do new things with our hands—basketry, cane seating, weaving, and knitting—and when I was in my teens, a home economics department was introduced into the school; a new teacher, fresh from the university, came to show blind girls how to cook and wash and iron. It seems unbelievable now the things I did not know how to do. I had never learned to strike a match, and I was afraid to do it. At our work-table in the kitchen we stood side by side. Mary Jackson, the girl next to me, could see a little, and whenever she lit her hot plate, I suggested that she lean over and light mine.

"Eleanor," Miss Hirsch said, "you must never do that again."

30

So she stood beside me until I learned how. We were using safety matches, but before I could get my stove lighted and put my match out, the flame burned my fingers.

"I don't believe I'd be afraid," I told Miss Hirsch, "if the matches were longer." So the safety matches were discarded, and a regular size substituted.

Miss Hirsch taught me to light the oven, but the task which took the most courage was putting potatoes into it and taking them out for testing. The oven seemed to me like a huge furnace, puffing its hot breath at me. I felt the same about ironing as I did about the oven. But all these tasks became easier week by week. I learned how to make pies and cakes, how to fry foods, how to carry dishes steadily, and how to do all the simple household tasks so common to the average person.

One day someone turned on one of the stove burners without lighting it, and when I went to light another burner, the gas exploded. The flames leaped to my face. Someone screamed. I turned off my burner and fled. Miss Hirsch found me in the corridor.

"Are you hurt, Eleanor?" she asked me in quiet concern.

"No, I guess it just scared me."

"When you go back to the class," she said, "make as little of the matter as you can."

Later, when we sat talking as we so often did, Miss Hirsch said, "Eleanor, you ought to be a teacher."

I had never thought of that before, and when I asked her why, she said, "You know how to meet emergencies, and that is important in teaching."

On another day we were making Jello. Of course, the idea was to get it cooled as quickly as possible. I put mine in the upper part of the icebox, against the ice, though Miss Hirsch had suggested that we use the lower part of the box. Everything went fine until I reached in to get my bowl of Jello. Then the lid fell down and hit me on the head! For days I went around with a white patch on my forehead, battle-scarred for disobedience.

Whenever I think of my training in home economics, I experience a feeling of satisfaction, for though it took courage, I learned more than in any other course..

Just as other young folks do, we put on plays such as *She Stoops to Conquer* and *William Tell*. Often my part was small, but sometimes I had the lead. When I was thirteen, Miss Harding chose me for the part of Mother Nature in a cantata, *Mother Nature's Festival*. I was proud to have the lead in a cast of more than a hundred, and I wished my mother could have been there to hear and see me. But she was working and could not afford to come.

The difficult part of the year for my mother was the summer. She always wanted to keep me with her, and if she couldn't take me to the first class hotel where she worked, she went elsewhere. Sometimes I helped her make the beds; at other times I dried dishes. She seemed to prefer having me play, however, so she bought beads for beadwork and raffia with which I could make hats and bags.

She urged me to sleep late, but whenever I did, a strange thing happened that made me afraid. The thumb and first finger of my left hand became numb; then the numbness passed to my other fingers, on up through my hand to the elbow, into my face and tongue. The fear of paralysis troubled me. As I cried and my mother rubbed my arm vigorously, I thought, "It isn't so bad to be blind, but I don't know what I'd do if I couldn't use my hands, or talk."

My mother tried to persuade me that my arm had only gone to sleep, but I knew it wasn't that. And she felt that it was a result of my childhood illnesses.

The summer I was thirteen, somebody gave me a white French poodle. Prince was "beautiful but dumb." His hair was not kinky like that of most poodles; it lay in soft ringlets all over his body. After my mother had worked all day, she would bathe and dress, and with Prince in one arm, and with me holding to the other, we would go for a walk. There was always a soda to finish up the evening. As the time drew near for me to go to school, I knew that Prince and I must part. One of the guests in the hotel wanted the poodle and she said she would send me a brown merino dress in the winter in exchange for him. I gave him to her, and I waited and waited, but the dress never came.

When I was fourteen my mother took a new job, cooking in a restaurant, in order to make more money to provide for me. There was no place to play where she worked. My sister had married, and Mamma wanted me to stay with Katherine as often as I would. But somehow I always wanted to stay with my mother. She would take me over to my sister's on Monday and promise to come to see me on Thursday. On Thursday I always went back with her. There was a family of seven children next door to my sister's. I played with them much of the time, but even that could not make up for my not being with Mamma. One evening I remember in particular. Katherine complained that I wouldn't do dishes for her.

"Oh, don't always be picking at her," Mamma said. "She's here such a short time." So I knew my mother was dreading our separation as much as I was, in spite of the worry I was to her.

As September and school time drew near, I did not want to go back. I looked forward to seeing the girls and the teachers, but I disliked more and more having to leave my mother. At the depot she was surprised to see me cry. I was surprised, too, but a feeling of foreboding hung over me. Back in school, I was wretchedly homesick. The days were all right, but every night for weeks I cried myself to sleep. In April my mother wrote that she had stopped working and was staying with Katherine. I recalled that the summer before I had weighed more than she did, and now this fact took on a new significance.

In May my mother wrote: "Eleanor, Grandpa has been sick for a long time. We aren't going to be sorry that he died, because he is better off." When Miss Avey, the matron, read the letter, I said, "I wish I could go home."

"It's less than a month until school closes," she suggested. "And you couldn't see your grandpa if you did go home."

"It's Mamma I want to see."

But the month was too long. Early in June the news came. I was in spelling class when one of the girls was sent to tell me that the matron wanted to see me.

"Maybe it's a letter," I said joyfully, rushing upstairs. But then I realized that Miss Avey would not take me out of class just for a letter. "I better not get on my high horse," I suggested to Sadie. "It might be bad news."

Miss Avey was waiting for me at the head of the stairs. We sat on the bench in the bathroom where many times before I had buttoned my shoes and waited to be washed and combed. I was older now and I combed my own hair, but it still seemed natural to go into the little girls' bathroom. I noticed that Miss Avey had closed the door. I was certain that something was wrong, and I began to cry.

"Eleanor," Miss Avery asked finally, "has your Mamma been sick very long?"

"Two months, I think." I wondered vaguely how much longer it had really been.

"Your Uncle Dell," Miss Avey said, "telegraphed this morning that you are to go home. We'll send you this afternoon." She did not tell me the real reason for my going home. Perhaps she thought my sister should do it, or maybe she felt I already knew. As soon as I reached home and Katherine told me about Mamma I wanted to go back to school. I felt that my mother was not really there, and though my sister wanted me to go to see her where she lay in her casket in the front room, I could not go. On the day of the funeral the house was very heavy with the odor of lilies, carnations, and roses. It rained just before the funeral began, not a hard rain, but a gentle sprinkling. Then suddenly I felt the sun warm on my face. I do not remember any of the service, but I recall standing with my sister beside my mother. Katherine showed me her satin dress with the lace front; it was the kind of dress I thought my mother would have liked. My sister put my hand on my mother's forehead; her face was cold to the touch, with a chill that I had never felt before.

"I thought you wanted to touch her," Katherine whispered as I drew back. For a few minutes I wept bitterly. But at the cemetery I did not cry. Friends of my mother thought it was because I did not understand. I understood, but a peace had settled upon me. I knew that mother's worries were over. Her tragic life was ended when she was only thirty-nine. Her stern father, un-

34

happy marriage, and my blindness could trouble her no more, and however much I missed her, I would never wish her back. "Tell Eleanor . . ." she had murmured before she died, but what she wanted to tell me we never knew.

CHAPTER FOUR

Security or Freedom

The summer after my mother's death, I spent with my sister. Katherine had made an unfortunate marriage. Her husband was twice her age, and his jealousy and drinking were unpleasant for both of us. So I tried to go elsewhere whenever possible. Sometimes I stayed with Sadie, whose mother was always willing to share the little they had with me.

In the fall, I visited my two uncles, Dell and Harry. Presumably this was a social call; actually, it was to secure money for my clothes. Uncle Harry talked of writing to my father for assistance, but if he wrote, nothing ever came of it.

I had never seen my father. Shortly before I was born, Mother had come home to live with Grandpa because my father's excessive drinking had become unbearable. Since then, Mother had never cared to get in touch with him.

Usually each of my uncles gave me five dollars, and after my train fare was taken out, the remainder was spent for dresses and ribbons. Sometimes, too, my sister made me a pinafore, and occasionally the older girls' matron at school bought a dress or shoes for me. Gradually I became conscious that there were two problems which I would have to face: my need for clothes and a place to live during the summer.

The next spring Miss Ernst told me that a home for blind women had been opened at Mount Healthy, Ohio. She called it Clover-Nook. It was founded by Georgia and Florence Trader, and had formerly been the home of the poets Alice and Phoebe Carey.

"I think you'll like it there," Miss Ernst said. "Georgia Trader is blind and came to our school when she was twelve. Clover-

Nook is in the country where you will have plenty of fresh air and good food."

I did like Clover-Nook. More than that, I liked Georgia Trader. There has always been a bond of sympathy between us, and I used to say to myself, "If Miss Georgia can found a home for blind girls, I ought to be able to do something worthwhile, too."

The old Carey house accommodated ten girls. When I arrived, there were three women already there. They were much older than I, and Miss Georgia called me "The Clover-Nook Baby." One of my tasks was to show visitors through the Carey home. As we walked through the house and grounds, I would point out places of interest:

"This is the manuscript closet where Alice and Phoebe Carey hid their writings from an unsympathetic stepmother."

"This is the chair in which Phoebe Carey's mother rocked her to sleep."

"This is the brick oven where they did their baking."

"Notice how winding these stairs are!"

"Aren't you afraid of falling?" someone always asked.

"No," I answered, as I descended on the narrow side of the steps.

"See how the upstairs porch is supported by three massive round pillars. The curved bricks in the columns and those from which the house was built were baked in the Carey kiln."

"The stones in the walk were dug from the creek bottom, numbered, and then put down in the same order."

"This is the old Carey well," I announced as hand over hand I lowered the empty bucket and guided the full one safely to the ledge.

"That is the oak tree planted by Alice Carey, when she was a child," I said, as I pointed to the tree opposite the kitchen door.

That completed the "Careyana."

That summer Miss Georgia's younger sister, Louise, came out to play with me. She rented a pony whose name was Beauty. Beauty was the first horse I had ever touched. When one of us rode, the other walked. Louise led Beauty by the bridle as I sat erect and firm in the saddle. In the driveway at Clover-Nook I used to ride Beauty by myself. On such occasions she would go to the edge of the drive and try to rub me off against the trees. She must have known I was somehow different. I was able to follow the driveway by the line of trees around it, for although I did not see them, I felt them as I passed.

At Clover-Nook I learned to do a number of new things, to make braided rugs of seven or nine strands, to print and collate Braille books, and especially to weave.

In August, Dr. Kilgore came to examine us. First, he looked at Lizzie's eyes: "The trouble is in the front of the eye, and perhaps something can be done for her." Then he turned to me.

"This is a different story. The trouble here is in the back of the eye," he said after a pause. "She will never see."

Although I had never really expected to see, I was stunned by the finality of his verdict. I slipped away to my room and cried for a time. Hope dies hard when it dies quickly; and I had never felt so wretched. Finally, I rose and went downstairs again. I felt better, more relaxed and calm. Maybe, since I never would see, I could do something worthwhile like Miss Georgia, or Fannie Crosby, or even Milton. Milton had written; I had always wanted to write. Again I had faced the inevitable; it hurt deeply, but the hurt passed, and a new hope was born.

This incident led me to think of my blindness more often. I had never heard the cause of it stated. However, I know now that infection before or during birth may be cured. State laws now require that silver nitrate must be put in the eyes of all newborn babies. Even now I dare not linger long over the idea that had I been born twenty-five years later, I need not have been blind. When I first realized the full importance of this truth, I was torn by spiritual conflict and bitterness. But I knew I must live at peace with myself. I must live in a world of hope and progress.

I must search out an explanation for my affliction which would be adequate to my spiritual needs. The thought that the carelessness or ignorance of a doctor had caused my blindness, brought only rebellion. To visit the sins of a parent upon the children seemed to me to detract from God's justice. My religion was based not only on a kind and loving God, but on a just one.

As Stanley Jones said: "Not what happens to you, but what you do with it, determines the result." Out of my reading and thinking grew the conviction that God had permitted me to be blind so that I might work out certain problems and make spiritual advancement. Blindness should not be a handicap, but a stimulus to progress. God then had sanctioned my blindness that my soul might see.

When I learned to weave, I could not set up the warp, nor could I wind it and string it through the heddles. The teacher always did that. But I could throw the shuttle and catch it on the other side, put in the pattern, and beat down the woof with a wooden bar. With my fingers I could feel the evenness of the edges, the firmness of the weaving, and the growing length of the cloth under my hands. It gave me a feeling of pride and satisfaction.

Life for me was like that. Out of my questioning and doubting, my rejection and acceptance, came the belief that life is a loom upon which God strings the warp and I weave the woof. I may change the pattern, the color, the texture, but the warp remains the same. It cannot be altered.

That summer at Clover-Nook presented a problem which determined the trend of my entire life. One day Miss Georgia took me into the little downstairs bedroom of the Carey home. She closed the door and I felt that something of moment was about to happen. Sitting down on the bed beside me, she began: "Eleanor, Clover-Nook can accommodate only ten girls. We have many more applications than that and I'm afraid there won't be a vacancy for you next summer. It's important to have a place to stay, and it's nice, too, to know that you will be taken care of the rest of your life. We have been wondering if it wouldn't be better for you to leave school and stay here."

I did not answer. I could not grasp the idea of not finishing school. Mamma had always counted on my graduation.

"It's a big decision to make," Miss Georgia went on. "I don't want to hurry you and I think you should talk it over with your sister and some of your teachers."

That night I wrote a letter to my sister, Katherine, and told her the problem. I asked her to come to Clover-Nook the latter part of August. I wrote, too, to Mrs. Chapin, my favorite teacher at the School for Blind. I couldn't imagine that she would want me to leave school and when her answer came, I was sick with disappointment.

"Dear Eleanor," she wrote, "it is difficult to advise you what is best to do. I know how anxious you are to complete your schooling, and you will be disappointed if you do not finish, but bread and butter is important. Perhaps it is best for you to stay at Clover-Nook." So Mrs. Chapin felt the same way Miss Georgia did. I knew from her letter that my feelings were biased; I was not sure whether it was the completion of my schooling that mattered so much, or whether it was the pupils and teachers or the school itself which made me cling to my opinion. At night I lay in bed listening to the dull thud of apples falling to the ground, breathing in their fragrance and hearing the wind in the leaves. They seemed to whisper of peace and security, of warmth and comfort, of resignation and lack of responsibility; in short, of Clover-Nook. But to finish my life there, to give up all my dreams, seemed unbearable to me. I pictured the little house and the children I would have if I married; I thought of the books I wanted to write and the lectures I wanted to give. Somehow I could not reconcile these things to Clover-Nook. I wanted to be free, to be independent, to *do* something.

I did not stop to think *how*. The things that should have been my first consideration did not enter my mind. What could I, who had always been looked after, know of neglect? How could I, who had always known plenty, understand poverty? How could I, who had always been surrounded with friendliness and willing hands, imagine a cold, inhospitable society? How could I, living in my own world where my blindness was no handicap, successfully compete in a world of sight? These questions I did not ask myself.

Over and over other arguments repeated themselves; security or uncertainty, seclusion or freedom, stagnation or progress?

When my sister Katherine came, we sat out in the swing. Miss Georgia and her sister Florence were there, too. Miss Georgia explained the situation. Then Katherine said, "I think it would be wonderful to always have a place to stay and to be warm and comfortable. I'd like to have Eleanor live with me, but it isn't pleasant."

So my sister, too, thought I should give up school. I knew if I decided to go back I would stand alone. I realized that were I to reject Miss Georgia's offer, I had no certainty that I could care for myself.

Finally Katherine said, "I think it is entirely up to Eleanor."

"We should know today," Miss Florence interposed, "in order to accept or reject our applications."

I knew that the time for decision had come.

"What do you want to do?" Miss Georgia asked. Her voice was so kind, I wondered how I had the courage to do anything but acquiesce. This red swing, I thought, as my hand touched the arm, is like the one that used to be in the court at school.

"I can't do it," I said slowly. "I don't know why, but I have to go back to school."

Miss Georgia and I walked back to the little white house, and Katherine and Miss Florence followed. I knew they all thought I was making a mistake, but I felt sure Miss Georgia would still be my friend.

"Whenever we have room, Eleanor," she said, "you can always come to us."

I had come to the crossroads; I had made my decision, and I was glad.

CHAPTER FIVE

The World at My Fingertips

Back at school again, the wonder of the place seemed, if possible, augmented. I had almost lost my chance to return, and I viewed everything with greater appreciation.

"Eleanor, would you mind if I ask you a question?" Miss Hirsch said as we sat proofreading her recipes in Braille.

"No, of course not. Why should I?" I answered.

"Can you see at all?"

"Not at all, now." (I was eighteen.) "But I could see light and color until I was eleven. Some people think that when you're totally blind, it's always dark to you. Milton spoke of the interminable dark. Mr. Foster says his world is pearl gray. I don't know how to explain it, but it's always like a soft brightness to me, even at night."

"That's interesting," Miss Hirsch commented.

"If I put my hands over my eyes, there is a darkness in front of them, but the brightness continues at the sides of my face. I've always been glad that it isn't dark to me. Maybe the brightness I think I see, is similar to what you experience when you close your eyes."

"Are you sure you can't see at all?" Miss Hirsch insisted.

"The last color I saw was the new cerise hair ribbon my mother sent me. Since then I haven't been able to tell when the sun shines, or when it is night, or anything. It's always the same soft glow."

"I've been watching you for a long time," Miss Hirsch explained. "When you go around the work table to the stove, the cabinet, or the sink, you never bump into it. Most of the girls do."

The work table stood in the center of the kitchen. It was

rectangular.

"I don't know why they run into it, but I can tell where it is," I said.

"But how?"

"I get an impression of its size and height behind my eyes and across my forehead, and when I come to the end of the table, there is an open space instead of the table. This image is interfered with if there is a great deal of noise, so it is somehow connected with my hearing. People call it the facial sense. Some blind persons have it and others do not. Those who do not possess it declare there isn't such a thing, but I don't know how I'd get along without it."

Then I recalled a number of incidents of my childhood in connection with the facial sense. As a baby learning to walk, I laid my hand against the hot stove. I wonder that the heat from the stove did not warn me. Either my curiosity got the better of me, or I had not yet learned to interpret this sensory reaction. If it was curiosity, it was dearly bought, for I still carry the scar from the burn.

We had a cellar-way on the back porch, and I was usually able to tell whether the trap door was raised or lowered. Once, however, when I was three, my sister told me that the door was open; it seemed to me that it was closed, and I walked in and tumbled all the way down into the cellar. Even then, I was beginning to rely on the facial sense, mistakenly, to be sure, in this instance, but using it nevertheless.

Generally, however, I could tell the lay of the land. My mother usually tied a bonnet on me to protect me from the sun. How I hated sunbonnets! As soon as I was out of her sight, I untied the strings, jerked off the bonnet, and threw it into a corner. Mamma scolded me repeatedly for this. She did not know why I did it, and I didn't either. Now, I realize that the bonnet's visor interfered with the functioning of the facial sense, and the hood kept me from hearing where I was going.

"Do you get a mental image of all objects?" Miss Hirsch continued.

"No. Doors are generally easy for me to locate because they

are sunk into the wall and are usually of a different material. When I was a little girl, I remember how indignant I was when the matron told me I could run my *hand* along the wall and count the doors."

"You were proud even then," she laughed.

"I can't always afford to be," I remarked. "One of the things that still give me considerable difficulty is the location of chairs. It may be because they are low. There are so many things that a blind person can discover through this sense—the size of a room, the presence of a building, the trees along a path, and a street corner. I can sense, also, a flight of steps going up, but I am unaware of them when they go down."

"You're pretty lucky, after all," Miss Hirsch concluded. "I've heard of the facial sense before, but I never knew quite how it worked."

I only know how the facial sense functions; I can not define it. No one is sure just what the receptory mechanism is. It may be kinesthetic, or it may be nerve impressions.

When there is snow on the ground, the world through the facial sense is completely changed. All sounds are deadened, and objects are not readily recognized.

At Avon, Connecticut, where blinded soldiers are being trained, the use of the facial sense is one of the first lessons. The boys are taught to become aware of a house, or a tree, an automobile at the curb, or a clothesline. This clothesline would be the most difficult to perceive by the facial sense, because it makes a thin line. Half-open doors are like clotheslines, in this respect. If a blind person runs into one it may be because he does not have the facial sense. On the other hand, it may be because of the thinness of the door, or because some noise has interfered with the operation of this sense.

The facial sense varies with the individual, and the more it is used, the more sensitive it becomes. Prolonged continuous use, however, produces in the muscles of the forehead and eyes a weariness which decreases the effectiveness of facial sensitivity.

In the substitution for sight, there is nothing of greater importance than the use of the tactile sense. As a little girl, I heard

44

that there was gray matter at the finger tips of blind people, and it is true that the hands of the sightless may serve to a degree as substitutes for the eyes. This is more essential to the blind child than to the newly blinded adult who is already familiar with the visual world. Suppose I had never felt a rose. You might tell me what a rose looked like, but neither you nor I could determine whether that image I formed was the same as the image you receive. But if I examine the rose with my fingers, I retain a mental picture which is adequate for my needs. It is important to show blind children as many objects as possible, in order that they may interpret the world about them individually.

This problem of interpretation is facilitated by the continuous and proper use of the hands. Most of the things sighted people unconsciously learn by watching and imitating, I definitely had to be taught—simple acts such as throwing a ball, holding my spoon, lifting a cup, or lighting a match.

The senses, which in blind people seem so much more acute, are made so by continuous use. Anyone who wishes to develop the sense of touch or smell or hearing may do so. People who see, however, depend mostly upon sight, and unconsciously close other sensory avenues to a degree. Velvet is beautiful to look at, but it is exquisite to the touch. So is it true of many sensory experiences. We do not appreciate how wonderful they are until necessity forces an investigation. My world is limited by absence of sight; yet it has become, through use of the other senses, a world in the palm of my hand and at my fingertips.

CHAPTER SIX

Outward Bound

The days slipped into months, and the months into years. I took so many extra-curricular activities at school that I required more than the regular amount of time in which to graduate, so I was twenty when I received my diploma. I had studied a little Latin, German, geometry, algebra, and a great deal of literature. I never was considered brilliant, but I was taught how to study and how to stick to a thing until it was completed. I came to realize early that I needed to use all of my remaining faculties to capacity in order to meet the stiff competition of the outside world.

All too soon I was a senior, and the simple everyday tasks took on a new meaning for me since I was so soon to be finished with them. Our class colors were blue and gold, and our motto was "We Finish To Begin."

Arbor Day was always a time of gayety for us. The senior class planted a pink-blossomed horse chestnut tree. Each of us dropped a shovelful of rich, moist Ohio earth upon the roots of the seedling, and it grew, in spite of our ignorance of horticulture. In the afternoon there were games in which children of all ages participated. There were also sack races, three-legged races, and peanut races. The day ended with a tug-of-war between the juniors and seniors; with a huge chocolate cake as the prize. I smile when I recall how much importance I attached to this event. The boys stood at the end of the line, digging their heels deep into the ground. The girls clutched the shaggy rope in front of the boys. We stood tense, waiting for the starting whistle. When it blew, it seemed to me for a long minute that the two teams remained stationary. Then, slowly, I began to feel our side drawing back; blood tingled in my ears; the rope cut my hands;

46

yet I pulled with all my might. When the whistle blew again, the junior class was over the line and the seniors had won.

That year Edward M. Van Cleve, the superintendent, decided to entertain the senior class in the faculty dining room, and as soon as his invitation came I began to worry. I had eaten with my schoolmates and with my mother in the summers, but I knew nothing about "being entertained."

The heaviest blow fell when Mr. Chapin, our senior teacher, asked to escort me into the dining room. If he sat next to me, he would see all the mistakes I made. But my fears were groundless, for I committed no social faux pas. My sister Katherine and her small son who had come to my graduation were invited also. But I laugh to recall that Katherine did not fare so well as I did. The beautifully appointed tables were too much for little Russel. Unfolding his somewhat generously large napkin, he announced, "Gee, Ma, these look like tablecloths."

Shortly before graduation, I saw Mr. Foster. He was one of the blind music teachers, and I had known him since I was five. I had not seen him in recent years for he was married and had a family. In the early days, Mr. Foster had given me a doll every Christmas.

"Eleanor," he began as I stood in the corridor waiting for him. "I was beginning to think you had forgotten about me."

"I couldn't do that!" I said quickly. "I wanted to see you before graduation."

"You know I'll always be interested in you. What are you planning to do after you finish school?"

The question startled me. I had not thought of it before.

"I haven't the slightest idea," I gasped. I had dreamed of lecturing and writing something but I had failed to consider the immediate future.

Mr. Foster had set in motion thoughts and forebodings which dampened the joy of those closing weeks. I recalled the many things I had learned to do, and yet I could not think of any way in which I could use them to earn a living. I remembered how they had told me about the difficulties blind people face in getting positions. Yet I knew I had to provide for myself. If I thought of Clover-Nook, it was without regret. That decision was behind me, and it had been right.

Though my senior year should have been filled with nothing but joyful anticipation, I was continually troubled about my clothes and the congratulatory flowers I might not receive. Ella's father was a minister and therefore could give her a dress and flowers which would enable her to make a better appearance than I. As it turned out, someone must have thought that I would miss my mother. She had once promised me a white taffeta dress, white for graduation, and taffeta because I loved the aristocratic rustle of it. So it came about that the school made for me a soft white handkerchief linen dress, beautifully finished with lace and insertion. The bodice and skirt were tucked and there was a wide satin sash. It was the prettiest dress I'd ever seen. The seamstress put it on me an hour before commencement and forbade me to sit down, for she was as proud of the result as I.

Before commencement, I went over to the library to see Mrs. Chapin. As I waited beside her desk, where I had stood so many times in the past to draw out a book or to get information, but really for the purpose of seeing her, I thought how happy the moments in the library had been. Mrs. Chapin told me how beautiful my dress was, and then, taking my hand, she slipped an opal ring on my finger.

My sister and the matron from Clover-Nook came for the graduation exercises. I had been chosen as a special speaker for the class and my subject was "Uncrowned Sovereigns," praising the teachers and friends who had served so long and faithfully. It was my chance to make them understand how much their friendship and advice had meant to me. When I finished my speech, I was surprised to find that I received, not one bouquet, but five. With my arms filled with flowers, I proudly accepted my diploma. It marked the goal for which I had been striving, but with it came the realization that my happy days at the School for the Blind were over, and I must now put into practice the teachings it had given me. A new life was opening before me. I had lighted the second candle for my darkness.

CHAPTER SEVEN

The Hands Have It

The summer following my graduation was different from all other summers. I did not have my return to school to look forward to; I could not stay at Clover-Nook; and I must, if possible, find something to do, for I knew I had to support myself. In April, before graduation, I had met Elinore Chapman, widow of the late State Senator who had sponsored several bills for the blind. She was different from anyone I had ever known. Her voice was clear with a slight French accent, and it contained a force of conviction which intrigued me. Then I remembered that she had invited me to visit the Association for the Blind in Dayton after graduation, so I lost no time in going to see her. Mrs. Chapman remembered having met me, but she was too absorbed with a new problem to do much for me individually at the time. She and Mr. Pease, heads of the Association, had the idea of putting blind girls to work in factories. This is a common practice now, but it was a new undertaking in 1908.

Early in July, three blind girls were given jobs at the National Cash Register Company. If only I could work there, I thought, as the girls talked of their good fortune. Since I was new to the Association, Mrs. Chapman could not know how urgent was my need. Finally Sadie's mother spoke to her about me.

"Eleanor really needs the work more than anyone," she said. Mrs. Chapman was perplexed at first, because the Cash Register Company had been willing to take only three girls.

"How about another factory?" Mr. Pease suggested, "some place where there is plenty of hand work, a paper box factory perhaps."

So Mrs. Chapman and Mr. Pease began their quest for a

paper box factory that would be willing to employ a blind person. Their quest ended with Aull Brothers. Together they went through the factory trying to pick out the things I might be able to do, but none of the jobs they selected was the work I actually did.

The day finally came when I was to start working. Will Hurt, one of my partially blind friends, was to take me to and from the factory until I could find somebody with whom to go. I reported for duty at seven in the morning. I will never forget the effect of the noise upon me. Only one who has worked in a factory can imagine the strain and confusion brought about by the din. There was the whirring of belts and wheels, the heavy clack-clack of the baler, the thud of hundreds of stapling machines, the roar of the bender, and the noise of dozens of other machines. There was the sickening odor of boiling glue and the smell of engine smoke from the railroad just outside the factory. Lily, the forelady, took me to the third floor. I held tightly to her arm and drew close as we walked down the narrow aisles past tables and machines and girls getting ready to begin their day's work.

"Have you ever worked in a factory before?" Lily asked me.

"No, I've never even been in a factory before!" I exclaimed. I thought of telling her how frightened I was, but decided it was best not to, for I didn't want her to think I did not like the place. After following a circuitous aisle we finally came to the work bench where I was to place tins in oyster buckets. Lily was very understanding. She seemed eager for me to succeed.

"There are twenty-five buckets in a pack," she told me. I had difficulty in hearing her because of the noise of the baler not far off. I felt as if a terrible monster were coming at me, closer and closer.

"Here is a hammer and tray of tins," Lily continued. "In one compartment are the eyes; in the other are the tongues that go through the eyes. You slip the tins through the slot on either side of the bucket, then pound them down with the hammer, and stack your buckets as they were before. It will take a little time for you to learn it," she said, "but you'll catch on."

So she left me, and I began putting in tins, pounding, and

50

stacking the buckets. When I had finished twenty-five, I put them on the left-hand side and reached for another stack at the right.

"I'm not doing badly," I thought. The other girl working at the same table pounded twice every time I did. How could I know she was pounding both sides of the bucket, while I was giving two raps of the hammer to one side!

At nine o'clock, when I thought I couldn't stay a moment longer because of the din, Mrs. Chapman, Mr. Pease, and John Aull came to see how I was getting along.

"How do you like it?" Mrs. Chapman asked, as I kept on hammering and poking the sharp tins into the paper buckets.

"All right," I lied. Somehow I knew I had to like it, but I wanted more than anything else to beg her to take me with her. However, I smiled and said nothing, for I knew that the hands had it. Life in the factory had begun in earnest.

The news that the factory was employing a blind girl had spread rapidly.

"Are you Eleanor Brown?" a girl asked.

"Yes," I answered, and memories stirred within me.

"I'm Mary," she said. "Don't you remember me at the School for Blind?"

"Mary Westfall!" I exclaimed joyfully.

Mary was partially sighted and had been able to get into the factory without assistance. It was she who had been tinning two buckets to my one. I don't think I was ever more glad to see anyone. In those early days at work she was like a good fairy to me, talking with me, taking me through the plant, and making me feel that if she could work there, so could I.

At noon the awful din ceased suddenly, and silence fell like a benediction on my ears. I wondered if I would ever get used to the noise. I never really did, yet there are hundreds of blind people now working in factories and liking it. At lunch time we sat at long tables and ate the sandwiches we had brought, and drank the coffee and tea which the factory furnished. Mary introduced me to a number of girls. They were all friendly, and I always found them willing to lend a helping hand.

On the Monday following, I went with Mary to the little

window to receive my pay. Lily poked a small envelope out at me, and as we walked out together, I opened it and found two dollars and a half, my first week's wages. The next week I earned four dollars, and then I went on piecework and made twelve to fifteen dollars, which was excellent pay for factory work in those days.

One afternoon I ran out of oyster buckets to tin, so Lily had to find a new job for me.

"I'm going to try you on folding hat boxes," she announced. "There's good money in it, and after you've caught on, I think you'll like it better than tinning."

The hatboxes came in several different sizes, from fourteen to twenty-two inches square. The bottom and two sides of the box were in one piece, scored with lines for folding; the other two sides had to be pasted in. But before the extra sides could be added, the box had to be knocked down; that is, the two sides were folded up, then four folds were made across the corners, turning outward. When the box was completed, it could be collapsed flat so as to save space in shipping. The hat boxes came fifty in a pack. It was my job to put in the six folds. I walked a little distance from my table, picked up from a stack one or more of the packages of boxes, and carried them back. When I had finished folding the fifty, I carried them to another place and stacked them so they would not fall, and would stay in fifties. The folding of hat boxes became my regular job, for which I was glad, though the constant rubbing took the skin off my hands. Lily wrapped them for me in glue bandages until they became toughened. I grew so speedy that the girls used to warn me that I would kill the job, but I never did. Sometimes when I ran out of hat boxes, I folded ice cream buckets, egg cartons, handkerchief boxes, and once in a while I worked on the bender. Lily did not like me to work on this machine, and I didn't like it either for the machines were not equipped with guards as they are now.

One day a girl working the baler leaned forward too far and her long braid of hair was caught by the machine. All the hair on one side of her head was torn out by the roots. I can still hear her agonized screams, and the sudden slowing down of the machinery when someone pulled the emergency brake and threw off the belt.

We worked from seven until twelve, had an hour at noon, then continued again until five. On Thursday, however, at noon there was always some kind of a program. Mrs. Charles Kumler, one of Dayton's social philanthropists, came to talk or read to us. I never will forget my joy when first I listened to her. I do not recall the story; I only knew that she was of my world, that she would bring into the factory each week the books, music, and people I was missing so desperately.

Though I was earning good wages in the factory, I never accepted it as my life work. In order to be prepared for any change, I bought a typewriter, and tailored clothes which would not go out of style. In addition to my purchases, I saved ninety-three dollars in two years and a half; I was getting ahead. I reasoned with myself that I had been educated to appreciate books and music, and that I ought to live in an atmophere of culture.

At the bi-annual reunion for the alumni of the School for Blind I was asked to speak on factory work. I tried to give a fair story of the work being done, and I believe I kept out of my discussion my distaste for it. When I had finished speaking, Miss Hirsch and Mrs. Chapin told me how proud they were of me.

"But I don't like it," I exclaimed. "I know I should be glad to have a job and I am, but I can't think of spending the rest of my life in the factory; not because I think factory work is beneath me, but because I want better things."

"I know it isn't easy for you," Mrs. Chapin said, "but we are so glad that you are able to take care of yourself. I can't believe anybody could have changed so much in two years. You're so grown up, even your clothes are different."

But I was not persuaded. I felt that my soul was slowly being consumed. Anyone could fold hat boxes. I wanted to reach up, to attain higher levels, and make my dreams come true.

Miss Hirsch had remained silent. Now, however, she said, "It's a long road that has no turning, Eleanor, and I'm counting on you." Somehow I found courage in her words, and I went back to the factory after my brief holiday with a plan for release forming in my mind. I would go to college, study as much English as I could, and then I would write! I knew I didn't have enough money to go to college, I did not even know any college that would accept me, and yet I felt I must go.

First I told my plan to Mrs. Kumler. She was enthusiastic.

"If you go to college, Eleanor," she said, "I'll see that you get a scholarship from the Dayton Woman's Clubs and help you in any other way I can." Mrs. Kumler was all I needed to solidify my plan.

Then I wrote to Edward M. Van Cleve, superintendent of the School for Blind, asking him if I might stay there by taking a couple of hours of fancy work, in order to attend Ohio State University, since both institutions were situated in Columbus. It took time to get a decision from the board at the School for Blind. It took more time to formulate my plan, so it was November, 1910, before I gave up my job.

"Lily," I said one evening as she came around to make out my time, "I'm going to quit Saturday. I am going to college."

Lily was almost too surprised to answer. "You're a good worker and we'll hate to lose you, but I'm glad you can go."

Then I knew I would be sorry to leave the people at the factory, yet I was eager to be gone. I had purposely given up my job before I told Mrs. Chapman, now Mrs. Eugene Barney. On the following Monday I telephoned her.

"I have quit my job at Aull Brothers, and I'm going to school. I'd like to see you before I go away." When I saw her, she tried for half an hour to dissuade me, but I remained adamant. All the things she pointed out I knew, and yet I was determined to take my chance. There would be little lost in the venture, and everything might be gained.

"If you *are* able to get through college," she finally questioned, "what are you planning to do?"

"Write," I said without hesitation.

Mrs. Barney was a practical person. "You will never be able to earn your living by your writing."

"Then I'll be a teacher," I answered doggedly. My college

54

career seemed to hang in the balance. I felt I must save that, whatever the outcome. After all, teaching would be steady, and I might be able to write in my spare time. I would not give up the idea of writing; I would let it rest. I was eager to retain Mrs. Barney's approval, for, after all, she had secured my job at the factory. Finally, she made a resigned gesture.

"Well, Eleanor, since you're determined to go, and won't wait until next year, let's see how you're fixed for the venture."

I had ninety-three dollars with which to pay my tuition (it was then ten dollars a semester), buy books, and pay my readers. I would go as far as I could on the money I had. Perhaps I could get through the rest of that year; then, maybe I could work the following summer. At any rate, nothing was going to dissuade me.

Mrs. Barney asked me what I needed before I went away, and said that while I was in college she would furnish my clothes. Her clothes were beautiful, of exquisite material, and fortunately, they fitted me. I knew if I went to college I would be properly dressed, and that gave me a feeling of confidence.

Back at the School for Blind, I found that my attitude toward it had changed. It was no longer the place to which I wanted to return more than anything else in the world. It was a means to an end now, and that end was Ohio State University.

Mr. Van Cleve seemed pleased to see me.

"This is indeed an innovation," he said. "The board is willing that you try it for a year, until you have gotten your moorings. If you're planning on being a teacher, you must not count on a position in the School for Blind. We are taking care of as many blind teachers now as we can manage. I don't know whether you're foolhardy or brave." Still, I sensed that Mr. Van Cleve liked my undertaking, even though I had sacrificed a good job.

"No blind person has ever graduated from Ohio State University," President W. O. Thompson told us, as Mr. Van Cleve and I sat in his office at the University awaiting his decision. "Yet I see no reason why you shouldn't be given your chance. For the remainder of this year we'll allow you to enter as a special student, and carry three subjects. At the end of the year, we will see

55

what we think you are able to do."

At the end of my first year at the University, President Thompson wrote Mr. Van Cleve: "Eleanor Brown has passed one subject and merited two. I see no reason why she should not be allowed to continue. I am offering her, at the same time, a one hundred dollar scholarship for three years. We loan it to the boys and give it to the girls."

In the spring of the same year, Mr. Van Cleve delivered a lecture, the title of which was "From the Paper-Box Factory to Ohio State University."

CHAPTER EIGHT

The Miracle of the Ages

My intention to attend Ohio State University brought into focus the question of Braille books and of how much use they would be to me in my college studies. This problem took me back in memory to the days when I had first learned to read, and to the change in the dot systems that had come about during my education at the School for Blind.

Why I should have been handicapped with blindness and yet endowed with an unusually deep love for books, I do not know. True, absence of the power to see intensifies the longing for things that sight makes possible; yet I am quite sure that my fondness for reading was evident before I grew to know that I could never explore the printed page.

Our home was almost free of books. My sister's few school books, the family Bible, and a Sunday School hymnal, my particular possession, completed our literary resources.

When I went to the Ohio State School for Blind, I was taught to read both Line Print and New York Point. Line Print had been invented by Samuel Howe, father of the author of the "Battle Hymn of the Republic" and founder of the Perkins Institute for the Blind, in an attempt to retain the appearance of the printed page. It could be read by any sighted person, but for the average child the letters were closely spaced, too slow to read, and could not be written by hand. The other alphabet, New York Point, originated by William Waite, was one of several dot systems formulated for the use of the blind. Nothing in my childhood gave me more joy than the books stereographed in this type.

When I was six, my reading actually commenced. No orator ever thrilled at his own eloquence more than I as I questioned from my Point text, "Sue, how old are you? I am as old as my dog. How old is your dog? My dog is as old as my cat."

At first, my reading was limited, because of my nervous condition. Books outside of class were forbidden me. Yet, ever fearful lest I get caught, I read the other girls' books. "Just one more page," I would think as I scanned with hurrying fingers one of Hans Christian Andersen's fairy tales. Yet, in spite of restraint and tension, I grew stronger and finally the library, with its delightful leathery odor, opened its doors to me. This made me happy, but I regretted that I must alternate a Point book with one in Line Print. For a while I bribed a friend to read my Line Print books for me, but the librarian soon discovered and stopped this practice. To my great joy there came a day, however, when this type was dropped from the curriculum.

Although I disliked Line Print, it held a certain fascination for me, as it resembled the printed page. If I could wish for but one thing, it would be to hold a book before me and read as a sighted person does. There is an added thrill, when singing, if I can help to hold the hymnal and give the appearance of reading. I have always enjoyed the possession of ink-print books, yet I was ten before I owned a real book, a New Testament given me by my mother at my own suggestion.

In addition to the volumes given us in embossed types, our teachers read to us each evening from books not accessible to the blind. In these readings, I thrilled to *Hans Brinker* and cried over *David Copperfield* and *Little Women*. When the regular reading was over, we would go to the superintendent's apartment. There, sitting on the floor as close to her chair as we could get, we would listen for another hour while Mrs. Smead, the superintendent's wife, read *Eight Cousins, Rose in Bloom*, or *Old Fashioned Girl*. Always I suffered from suspense when the reading ended at a crucial point. Sometimes I could not sleep and the teachers, understanding my mental anguish, would take me aside and reveal the denouement. The suspense of having a story read to me at intervals has been one of the greatest trials of blindness.

I believe I was in the third grade when I began to write. The reason for delaying the writing lessons is the difficulty involved in inscribing any of the dot systems by hand. This method can be likened to writing backwards on the inside of a show window so that it may be read from the street side. In the embossed types, the dots must be pressed through the paper from right to left in order to be read from left to right when the paper is turned over. The sheet is inserted between metal bars, the upper bar of which contains cells into which a small stylus is pressed to push the paper into the small perforations of the lower bar.

In Braille there are six dots which may be used. They are arranged in two vertical rows of three each and numbered down one, two, three, on the left, and four, five, six on the right. The number and position of the dots determine the letter or sign. For example, *a* is one, *b*, one two, *c*, one four, and *e* is one five. If two and six are used, however, *e* becomes *en*. It is apparent that by varying the number of dots and their position, a great many characters may be formed.

While in school, reading was my chief source of enjoyment. Though the books were bulky, they were light. An average volume was four inches thick and over a foot square, containing approximately one hundred twenty-five pages. In New York Point the Bible required eleven such volumes. Later, the size of the books was reduced and a system of interlining was adopted, permitting the use of both sides of the paper. Sometimes from continuous reading my fingers bled, but such a disadvantage was nothing to a child who loved books. If the story was especially interesting, it was a common practice to smuggle the volume beneath the covers and substitute hours of secret enjoyment for sleep.

During my school days, I was unconscious of the difficulties arising from the use of the two major dot systems, New York Point and European Braille. I can only recall having to read when the speed and accuracy tests for the types were being conducted. The controversy lasted for years and resulted finally in the adoption of European Braille. I have, however, never wholly ceased to read and write New York Point.

I wonder sometimes if the problem of types for the blind has been completely solved, since besides the Moon Print (large raised letters used by the aged) there are still five grades of Braille. Grade one is the simplest, grade one and a half being more complicated, while grades two, two and a half, and three are the most difficult.

At the beginning of the First World War, there were only approximately three thousand books in raised types in America, as the stereographing process was costly. Because of duplicates, blinded soldiers had only 2500 volumes in several types instead of the millions of inkprint books to which they were accustomed before the loss of their sight. The soldiers blinded in that war made the world conscious of the dearth of embossed books. Hundreds of volumes were copied by hand by sighted women, and the government appropriations for the Printing House for the Blind were substantially increased. But all this came too late to be of benefit to me at Ohio State University.

Years later, during a stay in New York, I visited the American Foundation for the Blind.

"How would you like to see a new kind of reading?" Mr. Irwin, executive chairman, inquired. I had no time to bother with new types and said as much.

"This is different," Mr. Irwin said eagerly, as we entered a small studio. Suddenly, I became conscious of a man's voice reading to me from a phonograph record. I recall that the voice was deep, kind, and distinct. What it was saying I do not remember. All I knew in those few moments was that someone would read to me whenever and as long as I wished. It was another candle for my darkness. After a long silence which I could not break, Mr. Irwin asked, "What do you think of it?"

"I feel as if I have been treading hallowed ground. It is the miracle of the ages!"

This miracle is called the talking book. The name is self-explanatory, but fails to convey the wonder of it. Sometimes I feel that there are no names or words adequate to tell what it means to me, and what in the future it will mean to the 75,000 blind people in the United States who have never learned to read any raised type. I would not in any sense underestimate the value of Braille. By means of it, I keep all my personal records. It permits a detailed study of a subject such as is not possible through the talking book. Braille furnishes, as it were, the necessities of life, while the talking book gives nourishment to the soul.

Actually, there are two essential parts to the talking book, the records and the reproducer. The records resemble phonograph disks, but have the added feature of running for twenty-seven minutes on a side and being practically unbreakable. It takes about twelve records to carry a hundred thousand word volume, the size of the ordinary novel. Like the embossed books, they are sent free through the mail. The reproducer is a slow-speed phonograph which can be borrowed from fifty-four agencies throughout the United States and its possessions.

At first there was a dearth of record books, but now I am reading an average of three volumes a week. As I write, the temptation to leave what I am doing and enter bookland with *Magnificent Obsession, Hamlet,* or *Gone With the Wind,* is strong. Surely, to the blind, the talking book is the Miracle of the Ages. It is my altar where I bring my problems and leave them. "And God said, 'let there be light,' and there was light for the sighted." And now, with the invention of an embossed type and the birth of the talking book, there is also light for the blind.

CHAPTER NINE

B. A. or Bust

My matriculation at Ohio State University was a landmark for me. I felt that I was again entering my own world. I had believed it would come to pass, so I was not surprised, but I was glad. Yet I was shy of my new surroundings and the many people I met. I knew that I was the only blind student in the university, but then, I had a goal to reach and so I did not mind.

I have never been sensitive about blindness. I have always tried to act as if I could see, turning my face toward people when I address them, standing erect, using the language of normality, and making myself a part of the group. Once entered at Ohio State University, however, I had a number of immediate problems to solve. The first was that of transportation. In those days I seldom went through the streets by myself, because of the nervous strain. I have always felt that I wanted to save my energy for other things. In the morning, one of the girls at the School for Blind who could see considerably walked with me to the car line, at the other end of which I dismounted, and was met by Mr. Chapin, who was then teaching at Ohio State University. He had been senior teacher at the School for Blind when I was in attendance there. Later, I walked with him to school. Between classes, whenever it was possible, I went by myself, but when I had to rush across campus in ten minutes, it was advantageous to have someone with me. When I left my guide and hurried into University Hall, I found the elevator waiting for me, which saved me from rushing to the third floor. The elevator man always looked out for me.

"Just in time!" he exclaimed, as the door slid shut. "I thought you weren't going to make it today."

"I don't know what I'd do without you, Mr. Owens. It's quite a distance."

"I hold the elevator as long as I can," he replied.

At Christmas, he gave me a copy of *The Rosary*; on a card he had written, "Just a little reminder of our ups and downs together."

I found a girl to walk with me to the car line when I was through at the university. At the School for Blind, I descended from the car, crossed two streets, and then went up the walk to the center porch. Crossing those two streets was the most difficult part of my getting to and from the university. Why I didn't feel I could go all the way alone, I do not know.

Another problem was finding readers. Usually I had three or four: a reader for French, one for German, and one for English. For some of my work, I used a high school girl, but for languages I preferred college students. I paid twelve and one-half cents an hour, and my readers were glad to get it. The law promoted by Mrs. Kumler for paying readers for blind students went into effect in time to help me during my last year at the university.

So often I was asked, "Eleanor, how do you get your assignments?"

"Oh, that's easy! I have the girl read as rapidly as possible, in order to cover the ground. When I wish to learn something, or have notes to refer to, I copy in Braille. Being read to a great deal makes it easy for me to absorb the material and to retain it."

I was also asked, "Are you able to get many books in Braille?" My answer was "No." For the few books in Braille, there was the difficulty of getting them in time, and finishing them in the period allotted. One summer, for example, I was taking a course in Shakespeare. We read a play a day, so I spent the entire afternoon reading. There was little time to get the book from the School for Blind library and get it back again.

There were, however, two or three occasions when Braille books were a godsend. When I was ready to study French, Professor Charles A. Bruce, acting head of the department, chose Fraser and Squair as our text, because it was in Braille. Professor Bruce's thoughtfulness saved money for me, and enabled me to study the grammar intensively. There were also *Caesar's Gallic Wars*, and a few German texts.

Another problem was taking lecture notes. I had worked up speed along this line, and I knew what to copy. Usually blind people write on heavy paper, in order to better preserve what they have written, but punching the dots into heavy paper on a Braille slate with a stylus is noisy, and at the same time exhausting; moreover, I did not want to be conspicuous. I was determined to sit in my seat and write as quietly as the rest of the students. So I procured a bound notebook, slipped my Braille slate into it, and wrote on soft paper.

After the first year, which was my proving year, I began to be more or less financially independent. In addition to the scholarship from the Dayton Federation of Woman's Clubs and one from Columbus, there was another from the Ohio State Alumni Association. Borrowing money from various organizations, however, did cause me heartache, for I was considered good scholarship bait. One organization put me on a program to speak without consulting me.

"I don't see why I should have to speak any more than any other scholarship girl," I protested to Mr. Van Cleve.

"You're quite right about that," he agreed. "The names of the other students aren't even known to the general public, but since you need assistance, and your name is already on the program, you speak this one time, and I'll see that they don't ask you again. After all, this is a business transaction, and you will be repaying the loan." He kept his word.

Yet I did not worry too much about finances; I was sure that if I did a good job, a way would be found for me to get through. My belief, frail as it may seem to many, proved true for me. Whenever I hear young people say they cannot go to college because of financial difficulties, I decide they really do not care to go.

Still another problem which had to be taken into consideration was my high school credits, as the School for Blind was not accredited.

"Your German and Latin you can take here at the uni-

64

versity," Mr. Chapin said. "I would advise you to continue as a special student; then, when you are a junior, appeal for credit on the strength of what you have accomplished in college." The credit was granted.

It was Mr. Chapin who planned the subjects I should take, and who saw to it that I filled the requirements. Since I had started in November, and because of high school credits which I lacked, it was necessary for me to attend summer school in my junior year.

I decided that since I was still interested in writing, I wanted a Bachelor of Arts degree, instead of one in education. Fortunately for me the law requiring a degree in education for teaching did not go into effect until 1915. I came in just under the line. I fulfilled the requirements for my B.A., specializing in English and languages. Instead of the physical sciences, I was permitted, according to the catalogue, to substitute mathematics. So I signed up for trigonometry and solid geometry.

Professor George Washington McCoard was different from most instructors. Every day he worked all of the problems himself. Then, at the end of the semester, he would say, "I have had my day; now this is yours." It surely was, for the entire grade for the semester was whatever we made on the one examination. By working my problems orally, I recall that I made a grade of seventy-seven, the lowest I ever made. He was delighted, and so was I.

I had three years of college French. The second year my reader was Mr. Otto F. Bond, an instructor. He read the French aloud to me, and I translated. I used to wonder why Mr. Bond bothered to read for me. Later, I found the explanation. He published a book on French phonetics, which was adopted by the Sorbonne in Paris, and of course, he was interested in how I would react to sounds without sight.

My third year of French was fascinating. My reader was a girl who had had the same course the year before and she knew all the fine points and difficult translations. I sat in the corner, over by the door, listening to the class mistranslate a delicate shade of meaning. As a last resort, Professor Benjamin L. Bowen called on me. I always knew it, not because I was brilliant, but because I had been carefully tutored.

I was keenly interested in German, which I studied for four years. One of the courses was Phonetics and Interpretive Reading. At the university there was a German Club of which I was a member. Miss Sarah Barrows chose me to recite a poem about a mother who took her son to a shrine at Lourdes to be healed. I would have liked the poem in any language, and I thrilled to it in German.

"I have never heard an American read German as well as you," Professor Busse said to me when I had finished.

I studied physiology under Professor Albert M. Bleile. He was supposed to be hard-boiled and was famous for hurling a battery of pointed questions at a naive class. However, I soon discovered his method. When he called on you to recite, which was often, if you answered and stood waiting for a further attack (we stood in those days to recite), Professor Bleile said "That's all!" and went on to the next person. If, however, you were eager to sit down, he continued his catechism.

At the close of that year, Mr. Van Cleve said to me, "Last night I sat at the table next to Professor Bleile. He told me that for your final you had written the best description of the eye and its functioning in the class." I was overjoyed. I learned a great deal about the human body from Professor Bleile. His explanations were crystal clear.

In freshman English, I was fortunate to have Billy Graves as instructor. Billy was a prime favorite with all the girls. He was dashing and debonair, and a real teacher. He allowed me to make up the themes I had missed because of my late entry. Each semester I signed for a course under Billy Graves.

One morning I was sitting in the "Gab Room" with Mary Store. A girl rushed up and said, "Mary, how would you like to go to convocation?"

"Fine," Mary agreed.

The girl continued, facing in my direction, "Do you think she'd like to go?"

"Why don't you ask her?" Mary countered. This has hap-

66

pened to me dozens of times, and I've never been able to decide whether the person thinks I am deaf, or that, because I am blind, I cannot talk.

When I was a college student, Oxley Hall was the only girls' dormitory on campus. In my sophomore year it was decided that I should stay near the university and President Thompson and Mr. Van Cleve suggested that I live at Oxley Hall. Miss McKinley was the housemother, but no amount of persuasion could rid her of the fear that something dreadful might happen to me while under her care, and President Thompson thought it best not to force the issue. So I roomed and boarded in a private home. I believe that Oxley Hall would have given me an escape from constant study. However, with credits to make up and long hours of studying to do, I didn't have time for fun in college. Yet I was content, for I was doing what I wanted to do. I was going to get my degree!

I saw President Thompson again when our German class gave a program at his home. I sang two German folk songs. I hoped I did them well enough to make "Prexy" glad he had admitted me to the university.

"Eleanor," Mrs. Barney said when I talked with her the summer before I finished at Ohio State, "there is one thing I do not want you to do. If you wish to teach, don't take another job. People are apt to think that you are located and forget that you plan to teach."

A blind person must depend upon influence to get employment, and though he holds it by his own merit, he is disregarded when he wishes to better himself. Since jobs for blind people are few and far between, the idea of a choice of positions is considered preposterous by workers for the blind. Fortunately I did not have to follow Mrs. Barney's advice. In the spring of my senior year, Mr. Wolf, the placement agent at Ohio State, called me into his office.

"We think," Mr. Wolf announced, "that if you want to teach, you might secure a job as an instructor of basketry or weaving in a school for the blind." I was furious! Finally, I exclaimed, "If I wanted to teach basketry or weaving, I wouldn't have bothered to go to college."

Obviously, Mr. Wolf was one of those who thought I'd be lucky to have any job. I had gone to college in order to use my mind instead of my hands, and I wasn't willing to shift gears so near the top of the hill. I believed that I would find something to do when I was finished.

In May of 1914, my German class was interrupted by the president's secretary, Mrs. Rausch.

"Eleanor," she whispered as she took my arm, "there's a reporter waiting to talk to you." I had met reporters before, but I had never been called out of a class to be interviewed. It was "Scoop" Reynolds himself!

"Allow me to congratulate you," he ejaculated. "You have been appointed to teach in a Dayton high school."

I felt the blood rush to my head. I could hear my heart pounding. I could scarcely breathe. Then my brain cleared.

"There must be some awful mistake," I protested. "I haven't even applied for a job in Dayton."

"No mistake," "Scoop" insisted. "Word came this morning. You'd like to teach in Dayton, wouldn't you?"

"Of course. It's my home town, but I'm sure there's a—"

"No mistake," he repeated. "You've been hired by the Dayton Board of Education."

"I don't know anything about it," I said finally, wanting desperately to believe it, but afraid to hope. "You'd better call Mr. Van Cleve at the School for Blind. He should know if it's true."

"It's true all right."

And so I left "Scoop," wishing I could be as sure of this news as he was. Back in class, I could not keep my mind on *Die Jungfrau von Orleans*. I recalled that Mr. Van Cleve had said, "It seems to me your home town ought to be interested in a girl who has put up the fight you have. They should be proud to give you a job." That evening I phoned him.

"Well, Eleanor, I see by the evening paper that you have a job in Dayton. We mustn't count too much on it. I went to Dayton in April, and talked with Superintendent Brown. I showed him your picture, and told him that if I were superintendent of a city's schools, I would not hesitate to hire you. He said that you should come to see him in June when you have your degree. That's all I know about it. If the papers are wrong, they will have to retract their statement. Go ahead and get your degree, and I'm pretty sure there will be something for you to do when you have finished. You've earned it."

After I hung up, I cried for joy. This was the most exciting thing that had ever happened to me. In spite of Mr. Van Cleve's advice, I did count on what the reporter had told me. I thought of it almost continually, and the thought kept me awake nights.

"Why," I wondered, "would God allow this thing to happen to me, if I am not going to teach in Dayton? Why would He let my hopes be bolstered up only to be dashed to pieces?" The God in whom I believed would not do that. Maybe He wanted me to have a job before commencement; nothing else could make my commencement complete. I turned these thoughts over and over in my mind. And always I came to the same conclusion. The reporter must have been right.

Still, there was work to be done, and finals to be passed. I must keep my feet firmly on the ground even though I felt that my head was in the clouds. Examination week was hot and trying, but the week of commencement was cool. I shivered beneath my cap and gown, but not altogether from cold.

I knew that the Van Cleves, the Chapins, Miss Hirsch, Georgia and Florence Trader, and my sister would attend my commencement. I really did not need a family.

We formed alphabetically on campus to march into the gymnasium where the commencement exercises were to be held. The "Brown" next to me was a boy.

"Do you mind if I take your arm?" I asked him, as we stood waiting for the signal. Mr. Brown said, "I will be proud to walk with you." In the gymnasium we went single file, and I kept my right hand just touching his gown.

The highlight of commencement for me was when I received my diploma. As I came out of our row, a cadet offered me his arm. Only a Ph.D. was escorted, yet here he was, helping me in my difficulty. At the side of the platform I released his arm, and walked across by myself. As President Thompson handed me my diploma, there was a ripple of applause from my friends in the audience. Memories swirled within me. I thought of the day when "Prexy" said I ought to be given a chance. I was glad I had not failed him, and I wondered if he noticed me when he gave me my sheepskin. This was the biggest moment of my life! I had lighted another candle for my darkness.

As the cadet escorted me back to my seat, I could sense the questioning of the audience, and I was glad that many did not know I was blind.

After commencement, I hurried to meet Superintendent E. J. Brown, who confirmed my position in the Dayton Public Schools. I realized that a new life was beginning for me. I had reached the top of my hill.

CHAPTER TEN

Historic Days

Mrs. Kumler, who had come to read to us at noon at the box factory and who had been the first to sanction my going to college, went with me to call on Superintendent Brown. The morning was perfect and seemed to herald a successful interview. Mr. Brown was cordial and easy to talk with. The atmosphere of his front porch was friendly and promising; there was the fragrance of roses and honeysuckle. Inside, someone was washing dishes, and a canary sang as if he were trying to keep up with the clatter. But those sounds and scents came to me vaguely, for I was listening to what he was saying.

"We will give you the title of coach teacher at Steele High School, in order to satisfy the board. You probably won't do any coaching." I never did. "We'll give you four classes—first year Latin, first and third German, and senior English. That ought to be a pretty good test of what you can do. We'll pay you six hundred dollars a year, if that's all right." It was more than I expected. "If I were you," he continued, "I wouldn't worry about my teaching until September. I'd rest and play all summer. To let people know that I think you are a good teacher, I'm going to put my daughter Martha in your Latin class."

I could feel the kindness emanating from the Superintendent as he shook my hand and said good-bye.

"Remember, Eleanor," he charged, "when the world began, everybody had the name of Brown, and only those who were worthy of it were allowed to keep it. See that you are worthy of it."

Before September, I talked again with Mr. Van Cleve.

"There are a couple of bits of advice which I am going to

give you, Eleanor, and I hope you will use them, because I think they have a great deal to do with your success. When you begin to teach, there will be times when you will need assistance. Ask for as much help as you please from your students, but never call upon the teachers. People who seem very willing at first tire quickly." I have never forgotten.

"When you come to something you do not know," Mr. Van Cleve continued, "simply say you do not know. Your students will respect you more for your honesty, and there are many things all of us have not learned. I hope you do not think I am giving too much advice, but there is one more thing that I would like to suggest."

"Please go on," I urged, for I knew that Mr. Van Cleve was more familiar with my problem than anyone.

"For awhile, at least, I would use a guide in the building. It will make you appear less conspicuous and people will not need to worry about your going down stairs or through crowds."

Fortunately I found Winetta Brown, a senior at Steele, who would do most of my reading for me, so I went to live with her mother, a couple of squares from school. This ideal arrangement helped to insure my success during that trial year.

In the beginning, I recall making two mistakes. Remembering my college days, I addressed my students as "Mr." and "Miss," much to their amusement. Miss Carrie Breene, one of the teachers, set me straight on that. The other mistake was that I gave too long assignments.

One time I engaged a college graduate, at Mrs. Kumler's suggestion, to grade my English themes. Before long my grader asked to be allowed to explain to the class her method of marking. I refused. I lost her as an assistant, but my students knew who was really the teacher. After that experience I graded the themes myself with the help of a reader.

The problem of taking grades was important. Since I wanted to have the records at my fingertips, I decided to make my grade sheets in Braille. I put the last name at the beginning of the line and whenever a student recited, I placed behind his name his grade. At the end of the grading period I averaged my grades myself and recorded the result on a semester sheet. When the students came to me with their report cards, a trustworthy one sat beside me and recorded the grade I gave her on the card. At the end of the semester I checked the cards to see that the grades were as they should be.

Joseph Henry Painter, who was principal of Steele from 1914 to 1932, advised us that one of the ways to make grading on the report cards easy was to use a special color of ink. I chose for my shade violet. James was delegated to purchase the ink. I had forgotten that James was failing and when he returned I noticed that the ink was carefully wrapped and in a box. He had stayed longer than I thought necessary, which put me on the alert. When I took the bottle out of the box it was wet. James had taken some of the ink. The first period I recorded James' "F," but later I took the trouble to have his report checked. Sure enough, the grade had been changed. That night I called his mother and when I told her what James had done, she explained that he had been such a "delicate baby" and that I shouldn't be too hard on him. In the morning Mr. William Werthner, who had taught for forty years without missing a day, gave me some good advice:

"When you want to complain about a boy, go to his father; about a girl, to her mother." It works.

In homeroom a student wrote down on a form the names of those absent. At the same time I recorded them in Braille. During my vacant period, if I did not have to take someone's class, I graded papers, filled out reports, or studied an advance assignment.

The first year I was teaching I used to come to school in the morning smiling and eager; at night, before I went to sleep, I wondered how I could go back the next day; but always there was the realization that, even if I wanted to quit, I could not fail my friends who had counted on my success. If my friends have helped me to succeed, they have also kept me from failure.

Alice Hall, a history teacher, was always kind to me, but it was after she was seriously ill that we became friends. During her illness Miss Hall was blind. To let her know I was thinking of her, I sent a half dozen daffodils. There had been many beautiful bouquets, but her sister decided that since the daffodils were few they would not overwhelm her but would bring a bit of brightness into the room. When Miss Hall's sight returned, the first thing she saw was my yellow flowers.

"Browny," she announced, "you need not keep your guide when you remain after school. I will always see that you get home."

There were occasions, however, such as Teachers' Institutes and banquets, when it was not possible for me to take my own guide. It was Ada Rosenthal who always asked me if we could go together. It was she, too, who checked my reports to see that they were legible and who hurried across to my room when a girl fainted or something else unforeseen happened. Since my first year, these teachers have been transferred to other schools, but now my own boys and girls are coming on as teachers, and I never hesitate to go to them when I want a favor. I think of them not as teachers, but as my students upon whom I can depend.

Once in my early days of teaching I was without a guide. As I was walking along I fell over some steps projecting onto the sidewalk and injured my thumb. In the afternoon, on my way home I met with the same accident, only this time I lost one of my shoes. I sat down on the step and tried to find it. I could not go home without it, and search as I would it seemed to be nowhere within reach.

"People will think I am crazy sitting here like this with one shoe off," I thought. But if anyone saw me, he did not come to my rescue. Finally I found the object of my frantic search and went gaily on my way.

After the first year, I was given five classes and my subjects were changed. Since then, I have taught Ancient, Modern, World, and American history, so that for the most part my days are historic.

"How do you learn to know your pupils?" Mrs. Kumler questioned, as we sat in my school room one morning waiting for the first period bell.

"That's a problem every teacher has to solve, and it usually takes two or three weeks. Yet, I imagine I know my boys and girls as quickly as the other teachers. I have to learn to recognize voices, but since I am accustomed to doing that, it comes easy. I use other devices to aid me and they speed up the recognition problem. For the first few days I call the roll, which is considered bad classroom procedure, but it helps to fix in my mind both the name and the individual."

I allow my students to choose their own place the first day, but they must keep that seat unless I change it, thereafter. In this manner I am able to look in their direction when I address them. Ordinarily, I do not have to learn so many voices at once; but by speeding up initial preparations, and beginning my recitations almost immediately, I think I often know more about my students by the end of three weeks than some of the other teachers. Yet that is as it should be, for all my life I have been interpreting through sound, habits, personalities, and character.

A few years ago a former student came to my room.

"I want you to tell me who I am. I had you twelve years ago."

"Jack Taylor!" I exclaimed, and he was more than pleased.

The children of my homeroom soon discovered my love for dogs. A committee of them inquired at the hotel where I resided to know if dogs were allowed. They were. On the last day of school before Christmas there was an air of suppressed excitement in my room. In the corner was the Christmas tree covered with tinsel and ornaments. The blackboard was decorated with balsam boughs. Pasted on the window was the star and the three wise men, which had been made in the art department. The air was filled with the fragrance of pine and the desks were covered with gay packages.

James Wilson, who was still a little boy, came forward.

"We wanted to give you a Christmas present," he said eagerly, taking something from his coat pocket. "The lady says it's eight weeks old and it's real smart." Into my hands James put a sleepy black and tan toy terrier, who cried when I did not hold her and so furnished amusement for the entire day. We christened her "Leo" for the huge bronze lion in front of Steele. I could not leave her at the hotel while I was in school all day, so I gave her to a friend who promised to care for her.

As time passed I began to build for myself a reputation for drives. I was chairman of the Community Chest, the Red Cross, and Christmas baskets. For its size, my homeroom turned in more than any other, but I'm not sure it is a compliment to be known as the best beggar in the school. I can still see my youngsters putting into my hands glasses of jellies and jams, boxes of pudding, Jello, and raisins, cans of fruit and vegetables, and bushels of potatoes.

Fred McCleary was in my homeroom. He was not an "A" student, but a sweet and impish boy.

"Fred," I said in exasperation, "I would like to give you a good sound thrashing." The next day Fred brought me a note from his mother. It said, "My dear Miss Brown, you have my permission to spank Fred whenever you think he needs it."

To my homeroom also came Frank Strickler, a little hunchback. He sold papers in the early morning and maybe he suffered with pain and weariness, yet his irritability to his classmates worried me.

"We have something in common," I reminded him as we stood together. "We each have an affliction which we must bear. We cannot help it and no one else can help it, either. It isn't wise or fair for us to give vent to our feelings, because we must live with people and we want people to like us." After that Frank and I were bound by a common tie, and his attitude became more cheerful. A few years ago Frank met me again. He is married and has a boy of his own, and he has learned how to accept his handicap and to surmount it.

Jewett Christman was an unusual student. He knew more about English to start with than most people will ever know. But Jewett knew he knew and was content to rest on his laurels.

"Jewett," I protested, "if you do not begin to study, I'm going to give you a 'B' this month."

My advice fell on deaf ears, so I recorded the "B" and immediately Jewett began working. I remember the poem he gave, "Antonious Pius Is Dead." I was proud of his progress, but when his mother came to visit me I sensed something was wrong.

"Is Jewett doing better?" she questioned, knowing full well

that he was.

"Oh, yes!" I exclaimed, eager to render praise where it was due.

"Since Jewett is improving," his mother continued, "couldn't you change his last month's grade to 'A'?"

"I'm sorry. I don't do that. Besides, the principal does not allow us to change grades."

"I talked to the principal," the mother suggested, "and he says it's all right with him, if it's okay with you."

"If I changed Jewett's grade I would have to change several others. 'B' is what I felt he earned and I still feel that way."

The episode had a definite effect upon Jewett. He treated me with much more respect, and when he was a senior he put himself out to do me a favor. Later in the *Steele Lion* he wrote: "Miss Brown was the first teacher in my school experience that made me feel she was confident that some day I might amount to something myself; that I was an individual, could think for myself, and possessed the right to have my own opinions and to express them."

One morning Miss Breene met me in the lower hall at Steele. She seemed much pleased as she told me that a board member was waiting to talk with me. I was not thrilled, for I felt it was not a social call. I had given his son a "C" the month before, so I was not surprised when he asked me to change the grade. I was surprised, however, when he requested to have it made an "A." Of course, I declined.

"It has never been my policy to change grades unless I have made a mistake myself." It was not easy to refuse. Board members have influence. But refuse I did, and I was inclined to believe that he respected me more than he would have if I had changed the grade. Later, when I asked a favor of the same board member he granted it, so I knew he bore me no grudge.

I have always been sympathetic with my Negro children. Many of them I have loved. It has often seemed to me that we have something in common in that we both work under certain handicaps. I remember with warmth of feeling Lilly, quiet, refined, and courteous. She always tried to do her work well and glowed under praise as if I'd given her something precious. Willa Smith, too, was always willing to serve in my homeroom. I do not believe my boys and girls ever thought of her color. We worked as one big family.

There was E. J. Reynolds, for three years a football star who brought Steele victories continuously. He was not brilliant, but a hard worker. He bought a history outline in order to learn the important facts. Sometimes he came to school without breakfast, and how many times he went hungry will never be known. The fall following his graduation he died of tuberculosis, and I, who had loved him, wished then I had realized how ill he had been so I could have helped him more.

I have always had an incongruous fear of mice. I'm not afraid that they will bite me, but I have never been able to bring myself to touch one. One morning when I moved the waste basket, I heard something flopping against the metal. I guessed instantly what it was.

"Harold, will you take this waste basket and empty it out of the window? There is a mouse in it."

But Harold didn't follow instructions. Perhaps he wanted to show how brave he was, so he lifted the mouse out by the tail and swung it around to scare the girls. As he drew his arm back holding the mouse by the tail it bit him and he was forced to let go. All the girls began to scream. I wanted to scream, too, but I wasn't going to let anybody know that I was deathly afraid of mice.

"A little mouse can't hurt you. Sit down and don't let the boys know how frightened you are," I ordered, as the mouse scurried into a hole. But although I pretended to be brave, I was the most frightened person in the room. For days whenever my hand touched something unfamiliar I was sure it was the mouse.

One of my students, Clara Distel, wrote of me: "She knows where the newspaper is, and who is chewing gum, yet she isn't different from others. I was in her class a week before I knew she was blind."

CHAPTER ELEVEN

Beating the Game

One of the biggest problems, and the one for which I feel somewhat responsible, is cheating. Students say there is less cribbing in my classes than in most of the others, but any trickery is too much to satisfy me.

Some people have the idea that my students will not cheat because I am blind. That may be true for a few, but the average child cheats whenever he gets an opportunity unless something is done to stop him. I have tried all sorts of plans; sometimes I have the books brought up front; sometimes the students stand by my desk to recite. Usually it happens that somebody makes a slip and sooner or later is caught. He drops a notebook or turns a page or leans forward to see the answer, and two plus two make four.

Jack was a mischief. I had taught his brother and I liked both boys, but I realized immediately that Jack would not study unless he had to. One day I gave a test. Jack sat just behind Frank, who made 96. Jack made 96 also. When test papers are read aloud, I know immediately when I have heard the same answer, so I compared Frank's and Jack's papers. They were identical. Without warning I asked Jack to take the same test over and I sat beside him as he wrote, or pretended to write. Finally he said, "I guess the game's up. My brother told me I'd never get by cheating in your class, but I didn't believe him." He failed for the semester and the next year when he took his history over again, he played a good game.

When the grades are recorded on the report cards, the students take them home to be signed. One morning I noticed a peculiar odor about the cards as I held them in my hands after collecting them. Immediately I began an investigation, for I recognized the odor of ink eradicator. Helen had changed the grades on her card, and though it took me most of the day to get a confession out of her, I finally succeeded. Yet I am convinced that some of the teachers attach too little importance to the problem of cheating. This is borne out by the fact that in college as well as in high school it is a common means of getting by.

James House was absent from school a number of times. Each morning when he brought his note supposedly signed by his mother, I noticed that the signature varied. Sometimes it was just Mrs. House; sometimes it was Mrs. James House. Investigation showed that all of the notes had been forged.

Mr. Jay William Holmes, who became principal of Steele in 1932, was accustomed to entering the room without being noticed. Occasionally he would come in by the fire-escape entrance. One day he saw a girl pass her paper to the girl in front of her. When I graded the papers, the girl in the front seat made 27 and the girl behind her 87. Apparently the little dullard was too stupid to copy. In Mr. Holmes' office I was told that this could not have happened in any other teacher's room. I did not dispute the statement, though I knew it was not true. A month later exactly the same thing happened to another teacher and she was not blind. I have always believed that the student who habitually cheats for me does the same thing elsewhere when the opportunity affords. Once in a while I find a child who is heartbroken when caught cheating. To him it is a dear lesson and I know he will not do it again.

Mr. Holmes' desire to enter our classrooms without being noticed bothered me at first, but finally I decided to train myself to be unconscious of his presence. Perhaps my training was carried too far, for one day while I was talking, James, who sat in the front seat, tore a sheet of paper from his tablet.

"James, what are you doing with that paper?" I stormed, for I like to be listened to and disapprove of note writing.

"I am taking a note from James," Mr. Holmes announced. I was embarrassed. That should have been a warning to my unconscious attitude, but I failed to heed it.

One of my classes was large. Three boys sat together in front and they were friendly and noisy and sometimes talked out of turn. One day I called on Ann, who sat right behind them. She was unprepared as usual, and began firing a barrage of questions at me. Suddenly a masculine voice countered, "Who's asking the questions in this class?" I have always aimed to be quick on the trigger and I thought immediately of the boys in the front seat.

"Never mind, smarty, I'll take care of that," I commanded. There was no laugh as I might have expected. There was only a stunned silence. Finally a voice announced, "That was your principal." He laughed and so did everyone else, but I was chagrined. I promised him a box of candy if he would not tell, and though I brought him the candy, the news spread like wildfire. Some of the teachers thought it was nemesis and some of them were glad I had made such an error.

When I began teaching, I had thought very little about discipline. I soon realized, however, that in high school it is an ever present problem.

"I don't see how you manage your discipline," Miss Freda Hirsch remarked, as we sat talking over my teaching experience.

"I don't exactly know myself. Maybe I am much the same as the teacher who is writing on the blackboard, and who seems to have eyes in the back of her head. Some people think that my boys and girls behave because I am blind. But that is not true."

"Still, I don't see how you know what they are doing," Miss Hirsch insisted; "but then you know a great many things I have never understood."

"Perhaps I can show you some of the simpler secrets. There is Martha, for example, who has been called upon to recite; there is an odor of peppermint about her, and her speech seems to be hampered by something being manipulated in her mouth. 'Martha, do you have gum?' 'Yes, Ma'am,' she answers slightly puzzled and embarrassed. Then I discuss the practice of gum chewing. 'It is such a bovine habit,' I explain, and immediately the entire class is interested. Two things catch their fancy—how I knew Martha was chewing gum and the meaning of 'bovine.'

They're much amused when they learn that the latter is 'cow-like'."

Soon I discovered that boys are the pacemakers, and that girls usually follow suit. At the beginning of the year a few boys are consumed with curiosity to see how much they can get by with, or to find out how much I can discover. William picks up a piece of chalk and begins writing on the board. I may hear the chalk rattle in the trough as he picks it up. There is a tracing sound, maybe a slight squeak as he tries to write on the board without being discovered. Elated at having completed his task, he becomes careless when he puts down the chalk. I may hear all three of the sounds, or I may catch only one; but in any case, he has no business with the chalk unless I ask him to use it. "My boards have needed washing for several days, William, and since you have helped to soil them, suppose you come in after school and wash them for me."

One morning I left my sophomore home room to go to the office. On my return I came around the corner before I was expected and heard a window stick clatter to the floor. "George," I demanded, as I opened the door, "what were you doing with that window stick?" Fortunately I had guessed right, because George was always starting something. In the course of a few minutes I discovered that he had been whirling the stick over the heads of the other students, as if he were going to strike them.

At the beginning of each new year, I must give a demonstration of my skill in detecting disorder. Once that demonstration has been successfully carried through, I have the united support of the class. True, there may be occasional misdemeanors, but usually the student realizes that the joke is on him and he is satisfied to conform to the rules. Throwing paperwads still crops out occasionally. One time, almost in the same instant that I heard an arm movement from the back seat in the last row, a wad of paper landed on my desk. "Bob, you throw like a girl. You certainly didn't intend to hit me, and if you intended to hit someone else, you missed it a mile." A laugh went around the room, and when I suggested that Bob clean the floor he could scarcely refuse.

82

Another time our band made a recording which was sold to the students one morning during assembly. As I entered the classroom, I heard a thin wavering sound; wavering but unmistakable. "King, are you playing that record?" I questioned. I knew there was no phonograph in the room. "Yes, Ma'am," he responded foolishly. "Charles was holding the pin, and I was turning the record." "Give the record to me," I ordered, though I was much amused. "May I have it after school?" King asked. "After school tomorrow." King's disappointment was keen, but no one else tried playing records without a Victrola that day.

In American History class Carl and Hobart sat together in one corner of the room. Hobart's voice was deep, Carl's was high; much like the voices of Lum and Abner. Before they came to class they must have gone into a huddle, for Carl answered for Hobart. "Hobart," I repeated sternly, and Carl's courage waned. Hobart had to answer for himself. That was tried only once.

Jim Weaver told me that once three boys in my class decided to chew gum to see which one would get caught. They were all caught.

The Becker boys were twins, and looked exactly alike. When they joined the cavalry, they used to do duty for one another, and the officers never suspected. Sometimes, too, they recited for one another in class, but they soon discovered that I detected a difference in their voices, and they stopped trying to fool me.

The wonder of how I can tell what they are doing keeps my students guessing, which helps me in my control of them. Sometimes when the warning bell rings, students are so anxious to be on their way that they stand by their seats, or begin moving toward the door. If I suspect that this is being done, I may ask someone a question. Without thinking, he answers from where he is, and I find out if he is out of place. If my boys and girls were expert in deception they might be able to get by with more than they do. Usually, however, someone bungles or makes a mistake, and the game is lost. It is seldom that I run across a boy who is a poor sport and tries to lie out of the situation, but the silence of the class in such cases confirms my suspicion. My students always support a boy when he is innocent, and you cannot

83

get an entire class to uphold him if he is at fault.

I seldom have trouble with cutting classes. There was a time, however, when Don was absent the first day of the hunting season.

"How many rabbits did you get?" I queried, and before Don took time to think, he replied proudly, "Ten."

"That's a good day's work," I exclaimed, "but you know you're not supposed to be absent from school to go hunting without an excuse." Don grinned at his blunder, for he knew I had trapped him.

One day Kenny was late for study hall. I smelled the odor of candy, and I watched and waited. Suddenly I asked, "Kenny, what are you doing?" and before he realized it, he answered with a mouth full of candy, "Nothing."

"It isn't fair for you to have candy and not pass it around, so tomorrow you bring enough for the class."

Everybody laughed, and Kenny agreed to treat, but the days came and went and still no candy. One day I insisted that tomorrow would be the deadline. Kenny promised. Sure enough, the next noon Kenny presented me with a large box of chocolates. He passed them to the class, and everybody began sampling his choice. All of us but Kenny had forgotten that it was April Fool's Day. There were a few pieces of good candy, but most of it was stuffed with cotton, pebbles, or some foreign material. Kenny did see to it that I got a good piece, however. Eldon was out of study hall when the candy was passed. When he returned I told him he had missed the treat.

"Why didn't you save me a piece?" he exclaimed, somewhat disappointed.

"You should have been here," I advised, "but just the same I did save you a piece."

The class watched in quiet amusement as Eldon plumped a chocolate-covered stone into his mouth.

I aim to play a keener game than my students, and I have always been able to solve most problems of discipline. The thing that baffles me is the tendency for children not to study. It seems to me if we could create a truer sense of values by giving more

84

thought to spiritual growth, we could develop more well-rounded lives in our children.

I am still pondering this vital problem.

CHAPTER TWELVE

The World Through Closed Eyes

Ever since I have been teaching, I have made it a practice to travel in order to see as much of the world as possible. The first phenomenon I wanted to behold was Niagara Falls. I knew I would not see it, but hear it; yet I was eager for the experience. I had read of the tons of water which fall tumultously over the rocks, the beauty of light and color, the roar of rushing water, and I felt that roar would explain the wonder to me.

From Detroit I took a boat to Buffalo. I had never been on a large boat and I learned a lot that first trip. The boat was so large I could scarcely feel the vibrations of the engines. On deck I could hear the water and feel the strong wind against my face. There is something magnificent in the rush of water and wind; it seems to force life and strength into body and soul. I stood on deck until the sounds from the shore could no longer be heard, then went into the salon where the orchestra was playing. Every time the doors to the salon were opened, letting in the sounds from without, I listened for the roar of Niagara, not knowing just how far it was from Buffalo and whether we would pass it by boat. Of course, I listened in vain.

A friend of the captain took me up on the bridge where I saw the compass. At least I touched the case which enclosed it. This case prevents fluctuations. I examined, also, the great wheel which, with the compass, controls the safe conduct of every occupant of the boat. Every half minute the fog horn blew. The mate explained that there were nine ships in the vicinity and only eight had been located, so the fog horn was kept blowing to prevent collision.

The next morning I arose early and hurried to the upper

deck to watch the sunrise. Sailors were swabbing the deck, and they looked at me askance.

"You aren't allowed up on deck until after sun-up," one sailor ventured.

"But I have to see the sunrise," I protested. Maybe the sailor wondered how I was going to *see* the sunrise. Maybe he thought if I *could* see it, he wasn't going to stop me. But at any rate I was allowed to remain. On that upper deck, away from the rest of the people, with only the water below me, I again listened for the roar of Niagara. I could hear only the rushing of the water along the side of the boat.

Suddenly, I noticed that the engines had stopped. Then a little boat came out to tow us into the harbor. I hurried to the lower deck to watch the sailors casting the ropes over the moorings and listened to the squeak of the hemp against the wood as the boat was pulled alongside the wharf. Then the gangplank was lowered and I hurried ashore to continue my trip from Buffalo to Nagara. I smelled the odors of the harbor, stagnant water, fish, oil, and paint, as I hurried to catch the interurban. Whenever the car stopped to load and unload passengers I kept listening for the roar of water. Not until we were in the town did the sound reach me, though not so loud or overawing as I had expected. Through sound, Niagara was something of a disappointment to me. Perhaps it is one of those sights which cannot be interpreted for the blind. When I took the Gorge trip on the street car, however, the roar as I passed close to the edge of the falls was deafening, and too close for comfort. I was fearful of an accident and relinquished other excursions.

Back in Buffalo, I decided to take the night train for Detroit. I had been on trains since I was a little girl, but I had never been on a Pullman. The berths were made up when I got on board, and I soon learned how to button the curtains to shut myself in, how to turn the light off and on, and where to moor my small pieces of clothing. For a long time I lay in my berth listening to the porter passing to and fro in the aisle, someone brushing against the hangings, and the rhythmic clack of the wheels on the rails. Yet I could not sleep. I recalled the boat ride of the night before. I had not slept much then either. After a long stop, when noise from the engine had ceased and the wheels no longer moved, I sat up astonished. Here was the same rocking motion I had felt on the boat. I knew I was not dreaming, and yet I wondered if I had been. Later someone told me that we had been on a boat all right. They were ferrying the cars across the Detroit River. I was glad to find that I was normal.

Mrs. Barney, who continued to advise me, believed that travel was an important part of education. Accordingly in 1917, she planned with me my second trip.

"I think, Eleanor, you should see first the United States, and later Europe."

"I want to go to Europe some day, but when I go I'd like to spend a considerable amount of time in each country. I wouldn't want to try to see it all in one summer," I rejoined.

"Why don't you start," Mrs. Barney suggested, "by making a trip East? Go by yourself, and learn how to travel alone. You can take a taxi to the depot, get a redcap to put you on the train, and when you reach your destination, another redcap and taxi will land you in the hotel. There you can find someone to go about with you in the city. There will be plenty of people who will be glad to accompany you for the trip."

On that first trip I planned to go to Washington, Baltimore, Philadelphia, New York, Boston, and home. I do not remember feeling scared. I recall, however, that I was excited.

Traveling on a train is for me just a means of getting some place. The only kind of transportation I really enjoy is by automobile or boat. I think I am fascinated in a car by the rush of wind against my face. The rapidity of motion, the sound of the tracing of the wheels on the road, and the exhilaration I experience from the fresh air, help to make it interesting. On a boat, I enjoy the rise and fall of the craft in the swell, the rush and roar of the water, and the absence of all contact with civilization.

In Washington, where I was supposed to change trains, I was not allowed out of the station because of the war, and because I had no business in the Capitol.

88

In the Pullman from Washington to Baltimore a man addressed me: "Pardon me, are you one of those who can't see from overseas?" Smiling, I informed him I was not. I can still recall his decreased interest and disappointment when he discovered that I was just an ordinary blind person. I was sorry to have so disillusioned him.

At Baltimore, I visited Evergreen, the training school for blinded soldiers of the First World War. There were nine men there, all of whom had lost their sight in this country. They were learning Braille and doing all the other things that blind people have been taught. It is fortunate that they are furnished with a pension from the government, since there have been so few things found for blind people to do.

After visiting Overbrook, the School for Blind outside of Philadelphia, I hurried on to New York, and to the Martha Washington Hotel. I smile now when I think that I felt compelled at that time to stay in a hotel for women only. It had its advantages, however, for the bellhops were girls, and after they were through working, one of them went with me to shows, around the island, and anywhere I wanted to go. One morning we planned a trip to Asbury Park. We were going to take the boat at the Battery.

"Let's take the subway down to the Battery," the bellhop suggested; but I demurred.

"Take the Broadway car," I urged, fearing the subway, and because she was escorting me, she yielded. However, we almost missed the boat.

I had chosen Asbury because the beach was shallow, the sand warm and white, and there were ropes to which you might cling when you went into the water. I am not brave in water because I was never taught to swim. Yet the ocean holds a peculiar fascination for me. I love to stand on the shore and listen to the booming of the surf, the waves coming in and retreating, each time a little nearer or a little farther away. And yet, as I am fascinated, I grow restless. I want to stay and yet I want to run away. Beyond me, farther than I can hear or comprehend, are great deep stretches of water which make me conscious of God's power and of his protection. I ventured in in my bathing suit, not the kind of bathing suit worn nowadays, but one with a skirt, modest and all-covering. We wore stockings on the beach and no one dared to cross the boardwalk in a bathing suit.

I never found the same joy and exhilaration in the waters of the Pacific that I felt that day at Asbury Park. I stayed in three hours, which was too long, but came out relaxed and refreshed and gorgeously sunburned.

Back in New York, I rode on top of the Fifth Avenue bus, hanging onto the banister as I climbed the curving stairway to the upper deck. There the wind blew through my hair and against my face. I could hear the bus wheels bouncing along the Drive, the jingle of the little bell as the conductor fed coins into the mouth of the bank. I still wonder what that bank looked like. Suddenly the guard boomed out, "Low Bridge." I wondered how low I was supposed to bend, but I didn't get hit. The Fifth Avenue bus was certainly an institution of New York City and I loved riding on top.

At 116th Street I dismounted in order to pass Columbia University. In the center of the court, upon which the buildings face, stands a great statue of Minerva with an owl peeping out from beneath the folds of her skirt. Suddenly I knew I would come back. I had to come back, and the longing inside of me grew until it took form.

After I had stayed at the Martha Washington a week, I phoned the Van Cleves to let them know I was in town. Mr. Van Cleve was now the principal of the New York Institute for the Education of the Blind. I can still hear the shocked surprise in Mrs. Van Cleve's voice, "You don't mean that you're in New York alone?"

"Of course, and I'm having a wonderful time." I tried to act as if I had been doing this sort of thing all my life.

"When you have finished with your wanderings," Mrs. Van Cleve said, "come and spend a week with us." I never dreamed such a thing would happen to me, and I was pleased but shy about accepting the invitation. I checked out of the Martha

Ph.D., Columbia University, 1934.

Between classes at
Wilbur Wright School.

Teaching with Topsy.

Topsy
(1938-1948)

With Carston Ohnstead and Ray McGuire
at Seeing Eye, June, 1938.

Miss Effie
(1948- . . . .)

Lecturing with Miss Effie.

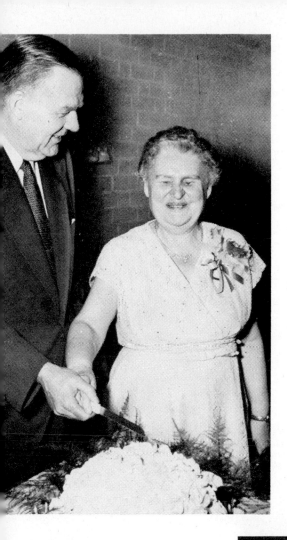

Sixty--seventh birthday celebration at the Dayton Art Institute, August 28, 1954. Superintendent of Dayton Schools Robert B. French assists in cutting the cake.

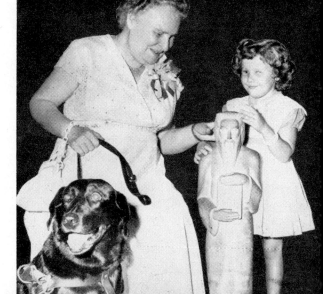

Viewing "Moses and the Ten Commandments" with young Carol Cooper at the birthday celebration.

Washington, went for the last time to the Little Church Around the Corner, and took a taxi to the School for Blind.

In 1917 the New York School for Blind was on Thirty-fourth Street. Outside of the windows of my room on the third floor ran the elevated. Lillian Van Cleve told me about the elevated and the subway, and so I tried both before leaving New York. I dislike the noise and the hurry of the subway. I always feel as if I am going into an underground cellar; the air has a damp, cool, earthy odor, but the roaring train coming toward me breaks the spell, and I am glad to run aboard (for it is almost running) and find a seat when it is possible.

From New York I went to Boston. There I visited the Sunshine Home for Blind Babies. There were children from the cradle to the age of six, and I can still feel the eager hands touching my dress, little heads leaning against me, and everyone trying to get close to the visiting lady. I must have been like those children when I was a little girl, trying to bring into my world through touch the experiences denied me by the loss of sight.

After I had visited Cambridge and Harvard University, I knew from the thinness of my pocketbook that it was time for me to go home. I had just enough money for my ticket, my incidental expenses, and my dinner. Breakfast would have to wait until I was back in Dayton. Aboard the train, the porter walked with me to the diner and found me a table. The waiter took my order, and though I felt a little timid, I was content. I had learned many things on my trip east, and I knew I would return.

CHAPTER THIRTEEN

Rough Seas

During the winter, if I have something to look forward to and to dream of, I work better. So it was that after my trip east, I began immediately to plan to go back. I would attend summer school at Columbia. I had managed at Ohio State and I could do it again, and this time I would be less hampered by the lack of funds. Mrs. Van Cleve made a reservation for me at Whittier Hall.

I registered for twelve points.

"How does it happen they allowed you to take twelve points? They only let me have six," one of the girls inquired.

"Well, I suppose they looked me over and decided I wouldn't be able to pass anyway, so they might as well let me have what I wanted." I passed my courses, however, and I was so taken with the atmosphere of the dormitory and the classes I attended that I determined to return in the fall and secure my Master's Degree.

Mrs. Barney came to New York at the end of summer school. For some reason, she seemed to oppose my undertaking. Maybe she thought I wanted to get out of teaching. Perhaps she wanted to be sure that my determination was sound. The night before I saw her, I slept very little. Somehow, I could not give up this desire which had become so vital. After talking to me, however, she decided to let me have my way.

When I had secured a year's leave of absence from my teaching I returned to Columbia and to Whittier Hall. My room was very small, but I was happy in it. On my dresser I placed a picture of Christ. From this I should find inspiration.

I decided to take my work at Columbia proper in the English Department, for I was still interested in writing and lecturing.

92

In order to increase my finances, I did some knitting and sold candy, but my M.A. was not to be won without a struggle, and during the trying months that followed it took almost more courage than I possessed.

One of the professors under whom I studied was Brander Matthews. He was then quite old, but as brilliant and witty as ever. I sat in the front row, absorbing all he had to say. In discussing the Baconian theory he explained, "There is just about as much Bacon in Shakespeare as there is in beans."

I planned to write my thesis on the rhetoric of Shakespeare's sonnets. When I asked him if he knew of any references on the subject, he chuckled and said, "Oh, you'll have to work that out yourself. There aren't any references on that subject." Brander Matthews was the greatest teacher under whom I had ever studied, and I looked forward to Saturdays and his classes.

For Christmas one of the girls made me rose draperies and a spread for my bed. I went to 125th Street and bought a small tree for my desk and trimmed it with candies wrapped in different colored papers. It probably was not a thing of beauty, but I inhaled the pine fragrance and was happy.

That was a long-to-be-remembered Christmas season. Mrs. Barney took me to hear *Parsifal* and though I knew the story, I was unable to follow it with the music. That, however, seemed to matter very little; the music was sublime and I felt as if my soul were being cleansed and uplifted.

On Christmas morning we marched down the stairs of Whittier Hall singing and carrying lighted candles. My fellow-student Margaret and I led the line. Carrying a lighted candle made me nervous, but I decided if the other girls could carry theirs, I could, too.

Mrs. Barney gave me an evening bag, a check, and a number of other gifts. In the afternoon we went to see a play. It was not especially good, but I liked the idea of being with Mrs. Barney on Christmas Day.

In January, however, something seemed to be wrong with me. I could not sleep, and my nerves were tense. Finally I began running a temperature and was sent to the infirmary, where I remained until June. Dr. Keyes, Theodore Roosevelt's physician, was unable to determine my trouble, so he called in Doctor Arthur and together they tried to solve my problem. Miss Breeding was the head nurse, and I sometimes wonder what would have become of me, but for her.

I was supposed to pass my examinations and finish my thesis before June. Finally Miss Breeding consented to allow me to try to write my thesis in the infirmary. I had done all the reading I could find on the subject, thought a great deal about it, and so I was ready to dictate. One of the girls came in each day and typed for me, but when my thesis was finished, I lay in a trembling heap unable to do anything.

"Eleanor," Miss Breeding said, "I have just talked to Doctor Keyes and he has forbidden you to take your examinations. We cannot be responsible for what might happen if you did."

Miss Breeding knew how keen was my disappointment and how much I had sacrificed for my degree. She found someone to come in to read to me, not Shakespeare, but Joseph Lincoln's *Cape Cod Folks*, and I learned how to laugh again. For some reason, Miss Breeding thought best for me to remain at Whittier Hall until after Commencement. It was to have been my commencement, and the day, she knew, would be difficult for me. With understanding, she left me alone during those trying hours. I heard the band playing in the distance. With the owl peeping from beneath her skirts, the statue of Minerva would be there, too, looking down on the graduates. Only I was missing from that huge gathering. In order to forget how miserable I was, I washed the breakfast dishes, and Miss Breeding's appreciation, when she found what I had done, made me forget for a time, at least, my heartache.

The next day a letter came from Dayton, from Mrs. Barney: "I do not understand why you have not done anything about your job. I have it on good authority that you are not on the teaching list which is to be presented to the board in two weeks. Your position is too valuable to you to merit such neglect."

In the fall I had asked for a year's leave of absence. I should have known, but I didn't, that I was expected to write in the

94

spring, stating my plan to return. Troubles never seem to come singly, and though I had postponed my departure as long as possible, I knew now that I must go home immediately.

I was quite thin, and with seven styes on one eye and much the worse for wear, I was anything but prepossessing when I walked, with Winetta, into the principal's office. Mr. Painter seemed surprised and confused at seeing me. I went straight to the point.

"I understand that my name is not on the teaching list."

Mr. Painter moved uneasily. "You did not notify me that you were planning to return."

How I found strength to handle the situation surprises me yet. It was just before noon, so I decided to act quickly. William Hunter, President of the Board of Education, lived three squares away. Without phoning, I hurried to his house. Mr. Hunter was a kindly Scotchman with a righteous temper, and when he heard my story his anger was profound.

"There is a board meeting at two o'clock," he said. "I'll talk to the board members and see that you are put on the list. You go home and don't worry, and as soon as the meeting is over I'll phone you."

He kept his word and phoned me at five o'clock: "I told the superintendent that you were not on the list," Mr. Hunter related. "He said that was right. 'Give me the list,' I ordered, and I added your name. At the board meeting I told the members what I had done, and they voted unanimously in your favor."

All summer I lay in the hammock in the sun, trying to get well. In the fall I went back to school and for recreation I dressed a doll for Miss Breeding's little niece. I made a whole trunk full of clothes, and forgot myself in thinking of her.

The following summer I went back to Columbia and Whittier to complete my work. I took a course in writing under John Erskine, who was not only versatile in writing, but accomplished in his knowledge of music, drama, and art. I also had a course in American Poetry from Mark Van Doren and one in oral reading from Professor Van Tassin.

I passed my examinations without much difficulty, writing

out my answers on the typewriter. I received my degree in November, but instead of returning for the commencement in June, I had my diploma mailed.

In the spring I requested from my principal a recommendation for a raise in salary, but he did nothing about it. In the fall, Miss Breene, one of the teachers, took me to call on Mr. Hunter, who was still president of the board. Miss Breene told Mr. Hunter that I was carrying a regular teacher's load of five classes, and a home room; and that I had my M.A. from Columbia. She said she thought the Board of Education should do something about it financially.

"I know that Miss Breene is a good teacher," Mr. Hunter said. "She would not come in your behalf if she did not think you, too, were good."

Our conversation took place on Thursday afternoon. In the evening the board met. Friday morning the new superintendent, Paul Stetson, came into my class.

"I want to congratulate you," he said. "The board has given you a $300 increase. I am only sorry there can be no retroaction."

Since that day, I have received my salary increases automatically, until I was being paid as much as any teacher in the system.

CHAPTER FOURTEEN

Nearer Heaven

After my trying experience at Columbia, I had no desire to return to New York. Yet I wanted to go away during the summer, for I had still to see the world. Circumstances caused me to decide to go to Colorado. I had known the Kauffmanns in Ohio. Mrs. Kauffman and I were at Ohio State University at the same time. Walter, her husband, had known me in Osborn when I was a little girl. They were so enthusiastic about Colorado that they wanted to share the wonder of it with me.

"Eleanor," Clara said when we were separating just before their departure, "we want you to come and spend the summer with us. The mountains will be good for you." I accepted without hesitation because I knew Clara's home would be comfortable and friendly. I did not dream, however, of the many experiences I was to have out there in the Rockies.

As soon as school was over I took the train for Colorado. This was to be the longest trip I had ever made.

The one thing I wanted to observe was the Mississippi. I knew that I could tell when we were on the bridge; a train always makes a different sound when crossing a river, a hollow, deep sound as if there were great spaces below. Yet, I might not realize the change quickly enough, for I wanted to see how long it took to cross; that would give me a fair idea of the width. To make sure, I asked the porter to let me know. Listening to the wheels on the rails, I thought of the many boats traveling up and down the Mississippi's course, of the thousands who have crossed it on their way to the West, and how much history had been made within its sight and hearing.

"We're slowing down for the bridge," the porter said. "There sure is lots of water down there." I sat up straight and tense, listening eagerly to the ever-lengthening crossing. This was much more exciting than tunnelling under the Hudson with the metallic roar in your ears and the fear of suffocation gripping you. Here on the banks of the Mississippi, I was beginning to feel the wide open spaces and the freedom that lay beyond. With the river behind me, I settled back to sleep a little and think.

"When you reach Denver," the porter informed me, "you'll be a mile high, 5,280 feet. Thirty miles from Denver are the Rockies. There's a lot of rock in those mountains."

Mountains, like the ocean, fascinate me. They seem to stand alone, and yet they seem to belong to me. I had felt the mountains on the maps in geography, rough raised stretches. I had also crossed the mountains in the east, but the Rockies were the real thing. Yet I was not prepared for the changes I noticed when I took the train from Denver to Boulder. The sun was warm when I was in it, but when I was out of it, the air was dry and cool. I felt an exhilaration which I had never before experienced.

Clara was waiting for me with her two children, Jimmy and Louise, at the station. The Kauffmanns had bought a large house looking toward the Rockies, for Boulder is just at the foot of the mountains. I was so pleased with the climate that I decided to sleep on the back porch, out in the open. I wanted to get air and sunshine into my system, in order to store them up for the next winter. The Kauffmann home was attractive, Jimmy and Louise were interesting, and Mrs. Kauffmann was a wonderful cook. Walter, whose power of description was paramount, made Colorado and its scenery come alive to me.

Boulder and the surrounding country was a new world. There were so many experiences I had not had. All of them intrigued me, and I tried to enjoy them as nearly as possible first hand. I awakened each morning as soon as it was light. It seemed as if the light penetrated through the particles of my body, irradiating them.

The first morning after my arrival, I heard a strange "hee-haw."

"Did you hear our Colorado canaries?" Clara asked at

98

breakfast.

"Well, if I did I didn't recognize them, for I know very little about birds."

"They're burros," Jimmy laughed. "Let's take a ride on them while you're here." I agreed, though I had my misgivings as to the venture.

"They"re perfectly safe," Walter assured me. "They're dependable and gentle and go at a slow, easy gait."

That afternoon we rented three burros, for Jimmy, Louise, and me. For the occasion I bought a middy and knickers, and I felt a veritable part of Colorado. Jimmy brought the burro alongside the porch. I climbed onto his back holding on for dear life as he ambled slowly down the street, following the other two burros. The ride was great fun, though I felt it for days.

In Boulder, when I came to a street crossing, I did not step down, but walked across a metal plate. I could hear water gurgling beneath it, so I asked Walter what it was.

"Oh, that's the irrigation ditch," he explained. "The water comes down from the mountains, and when you want to soak your garden, you lift out a brick which opens the ditch." I thought of the irrigation of ancient Egypt, and how similar this was. It must take a lot of water for living in Boulder. But there seems to be a lot, with the nearby creek rushing down the canyon, as if in search of freedom and adventure.

That canyon held a peculiar fascination for me. It seemed like a great high-walled corridor with every sound intensified and reverberated. Many times we drove up the canyon with the car almost suspended, like a rocking chair tilted backward. We had to go fast in order to make the grade. We kept going up and up and up until I wondered if it would ever end. If we had stopped the car, we could have touched the mountain wall that seemed to reach almost to infinity; but going up we had the right of way, so we kept moving. Coming down, however, driving on the creek side, I shivered a little when I thought of the water so close to me. If two cars try to pass where there is room for only one, the car on the mountain side has the right of way, and more than one car has gone into the creek.

Just outside of Boulder is Flagstaff Mountain.

"We can drive up in a car," Walter suggested, "and I'm sure I can guide you so that you can climb down. Then you'll know just what mountain climbing is. It's a three-mile hike, and I think that's enough for a start."

We drove up to the top of Flagstaff. I was fearful for our safety when we stopped and backed in order to complete the S-curves. I breathed a sigh of relief, however, when we reached the top and I stood on the highest rock to survey our surroundings. I had the slightest feeling that I might fall off and roll down the mountain, but Walter reassured me. None of the sounds of civilization came up to me and the warmth of the sun on my face and the wind in my hair made heaven seem very near and earth remote. I could feel God's presence in the majesty and strength of these mountains and I breathed in the peace and isolation of the place.

Lunch on a rock was delightful, with Clara's homemade bread, fried chicken, and angel food cake. After lunch we rested on the rocks, took pictures, and then we began our slow descent. Walter took my hand.

"Fasten your heels firmly in the ground," he said, "and we'll slide for about three feet. Now with your right foot, find a stone about a foot down, now another stone with your left foot." So we went forward and down, picking every step and taking plenty of time. If it seemed to me the longest three miles I had ever tramped, it must have been much more trying for Walter. Gradually the sounds of civilization began to come up to me, indistinguishable and inseparable at first, then taking on individuality and relationships. I was glad to hear them, for I knew that our descent was coming to an end, but I was sorry to leave behind the peace of Flagstaff Mountain. When I climb another mountain, I'm going to try hiking up. It always seems easier to ascend, rather than descend, a slope.

Listening to the wind in Colorado was a new experience for me. In the town it blew soft as the sound of rustling leaves, but off in the distance, I could hear a mighty roar. It was the wind in the canyon. I used to listen to it, wondering how far it had come, fearing its power, yet fascinated by the wonder of it. Somehow, I always thought of God when I heard the wind in the mountains.

So the summer passed with trips and picnics and finally my stay at Boulder was over, but we had planned another summer there when I could attend the University of Colorado and do some studying as well as sightseeing.

The next year when I returned, I stayed with Mrs. Charles Pratt who lived within easy walking distance of the University. In the morning I took two history courses. In the afternoon I studied and in the evening I rested and enjoyed the calm of my surroundings. At night I lay in my bed and listened to the creek just about twenty feet from my window. Sometimes I could scarcely hear its murmur; other times it went roaring on its way, drowning out other sounds.

For seven summers I went to Boulder. I always felt attracted to the place, to the mountains reaching strong arms into the sky, to the canyons with their high walls, and to the people with their friendliness and fellowship. Then the doctor said that the altitude was too high for me, and I came away with a feeling of regret. Yet I still believe that someday I will return to the peace of those mountain tops, a little nearer heaven—nearer God.

CHAPTER FIFTEEN

The Moot Question

While I was in high school, I often thought of marriage and children of my own. I liked boys, and they often came to me with their problems and their confidences. There seemed to be a bond between us.

I do not know why as a young girl I did not marry. My inclinations were certainly in that direction, and it would have solved my problem of a home. Perhaps I was too sheltered, but this is hardly the reason, for many of my friends from the School for Blind did marry. I was devoted to Mrs. Barney. Her opinions meant a great deal to me, and though she never said so, I gained the impression that she did not approve of blind marriages; yet if I had met someone I loved, I believe she could not have influenced me.

I was awkward and ill at ease in the company of boys who could see, as my adolescence was spent almost completely with the blind.

"I cannot feel," Mrs. Chapin said as we sat talking of my future, "that you should marry someone who does not see. There are many successful blind marriages, but I do not think you should plan on that as a solution to your problem, especially as you have no one in particular in mind."

"I don't believe I approve of blind marriages myself, and where there are children, it doesn't seem to me to be fair."

"The likelihood of your marrying someone who can see," Mrs. Chapin continued, "is slight."

After I had talked with Mrs. Chapin, my mind was cluttered up with the questions: Should blind people marry? Should a blind person marry someone who can see? Should they have children? While I was trying to find the answers, my career got in the way.

In the beginning, I thought I was opposed to blind people marrying. It seemed to me it was only multiplying difficulties. Yet through observation, I have grown to believe that my viewpoint was incorrect. One of the dearest joys of marriage would be companionship, and two blind people bound together by a common misfortune and by an equally common understanding can and do enjoy many happy years together. A marriage between blind people may be an economy of service. The person who helps one often assists the other. Blind people are certainly entitled to as much happiness as their sighted fellows. I know of many blind marriages that have been a success, and I have known few that have failed.

It frequently happens that a blind man marries a sighted woman, especially a woman who has strong maternal inclinations. This may or may not be a marriage of convenience. As a rule, the husband provides a good living for his wife, and she in turn furnishes the vision necessary to his work. On the other hand, a blind girl's chances for marrying a sighted man are few. I know of one case where the girl was extraordinarily beautiful, and another where the girl had money; but these are exceptions rather than the rule. When a man who can see does marry a blind girl, he is apt to tire of his bargain.

The marriage that seems most practicable is that between a totally blind person, and one who can see partially. I am thinking of Ted and Hattie, of Katherine and Will, friends of mine who are happily married and who have this ratio of disability. Katherine, who is totally blind, keeps house for Will, a music teacher who can see slightly. He is able to give Katherine the guidance necessary to get about on the street.

The question of blind people having children is of greatest importance. Of course, where there is a tendency to inheritance, the answer is definitely "No." I am not so concerned about the mother not being able to care for the child, but it seems to me that a child whose parents are blind must accept a great deal of responsibility. Yet when I think of Hope, the daughter of my playmate Sadie, I know that my view has changed with time. Hope's parents were both blind, but she has perfect vision. She was a lovable child and spent much time doing thoughtful little services for her parents and their blind friends.

I once met a girl in Canada whose parents were blind, and I asked her if that fact had made any difference.

"Oh, no!" she exclaimed. "I have a wonderful father and mother. They adopted me when I was a baby. I feel that I can never repay them or be grateful enough for their loving care and kindness. I am so proud of them."

Maybe, after all, the problem of blind marriages is an individual one. The questions should be answered, not from the standpoint of blindness, but of capability. I know of sighted people who have made poor parents, and so if blind people fail, it may not be due to the fact that they are blind but that they are irresponsible.

The third year of my teaching experience, I went to live with Mr. and Mrs. Lester Schaeffer. They maintained a boarding house above the average, including in the family those of us who paid for the privilege of staying there. Just before Christmas that year, Mrs. Schaeffer's daughter, Mary Mitchell, came home with her baby, Martha Jane. So long as Martha Jane was there, my problems at school were nothing, for I loved this baby and it was a joy to help care for her.

When Martha Jane was just twelve months old, she was flower girl at her aunt's wedding and carried a basket of Shasta daisies. She was like a flower herself, with her gold hair, blue eyes, and winning smile. After she had performed her part and said, "Oh, pretee," when she saw the flowers, it was I who carried her to bed, took off her dainty dress, and sang to her as she dropped to sleep. The two years I spent with Martha Jane were filled with the most continuous and the deepest contentment I have ever known.

But Martha Jane moved to Massachusetts, and for many years I was without a baby to love until I found Mary Lou Weimer. When I first knew Mary Lou, she was eleven months old. Surrounded by flowers, birds, dogs, and other animals, she lived in a white farm house and was blessed with devoted parents. Life for Mary Lou was wonderful, and I have been privileged to share it with her. As a baby, Mary Lou refused to sit on anyone's lap, but when I came I could hold her for hours and sing to her and she never seemed to grow tired.

"I'd give anything if I could sit and hold Mary Lou as you do," her father used to say, but she never was quiet enough for anyone else to manage it. Mary Lou's loyalty to me has grown with her years. She would like me to stop teaching and come and live with her. When I tell her that she would not have so many clothes if I did, she says she would not care. She is twenty now, and when I visit her, it is her baby I rock instead of Mary Lou.

I have derived a great deal of pleasure from knitting sweaters and buying clothes and toys for the children I love. Now there is nine-year-old Nancy Garst who likes ribbons and dresses for school; and Carolyn Anderson, Hope's teen-age daughter, who is returning my little kindnesses to her by doing things for me. If I don't have much money when I am old, I have enjoyed the love and gratitude of these children who, although they are not mine, have become a veritable part of me.

Sometimes I wonder if I have ever really been in love. I know there was a time when I seemed to be walking on air while my heart sang, and somehow I feel that I have loved.

Before I began teaching, Mrs. Barney had married a man twice her age and yet it never occurred to me that one of my students might fall in love with me.

Gerald was always doing thoughtful little things for me— erasing the blackboards, picking up my mail at the office, running errands for me, or driving me around in my car. (During the depression I bought a Pontiac for $300.) While Gerald was in high school and college I never sensed that he had any reason other than friendliness for showering these little attentions on me. Yet I was not really surprised when he told a friend in my presence that he would have married me when he finished high school except for the difference in our ages. As time passed, that difference seemed to become less and less important. Gradually

I grew to feel that he was only waiting for me to give my consent, yet there were other things that I had to consider. I did not want to give up my career. We were both extravagant. I was almost too old to have children. I was blind. This last fact to me was most important, but Gerald never seemed to consider it. Perhaps it was his failure to recognize my limitation that made it all the more important to me.

I wanted marriage and a home, but I found myself thinking of Gerald first. Then he joined the Air Force, and when I heard he was a prisoner of war in Germany I wondered if I had made a mistake and allowed happiness to slip from my grasp. Yet when Gerald returned well and strong I still could not consent to our marriage. He told me of a girl he had met in Texas, and I felt he was asking me to decide once and for all. I advised him to marry her.

Even now I do not know whether my choice was the right one. I am older now, and companionship is a precious thing.

CHAPTER SIXTEEN

I Go Domestic

From the time I was six years old, I have never had a permanent home. Since taking a street car to and from school was inconvenient, because I thought I had to be helped onto the car and met at the other end, I decided, when I began teaching, to find a place within walking distance of school. This would enable me to be on time and would give me the requisite exercise.

Anyone who has lived in a private home knows that the problem is a difficult one. The people with whom you care to live do not wish to have the privacy of their home disturbed by a stranger. The families who are willing to give board and room as a rule have little to contribute mentally and spiritually. The fact that I was blind caused some prospective landladies to refuse me. I soon discovered that I could not be too particular. Yet the place where I spent my leisure, where I ate and slept and made friends, was too important to slight. For a time I lived in one of the beautiful old homes of Dayton. Mrs. Effie Pfoutz, a woman of culture, lived there too, and I used to spend most of my evenings with her, reading French or some of the best books in English. It was Mrs. Pfoutz, however, who persuaded me to make a change. So it happened that I went to live with Mr. and Mrs. Schaeffer and Martha Jane. They had no hesitation about accepting me. They had a niece who was blind.

Mrs. Schaeffer furnished breakfast for her roomers, and for dinner in the evening people came in from the outside, also. There were usually twelve of us, and with the baby to liven things up, we were a gay party. I stayed with the Schaeffers many years, until they moved to Massachusetts.

In the interim, Winetta Brown, the girl who had helped me

the first year I taught, had married and moved to an apartment of her own. Her landlady boasted of having known me as a child and told stories of my precocity. Winetta suggested that I come and board with her. She lived about three squares from school, and the arrangement seemed convenient. At the end of the month, however, when Winetta went to pay the rent, her landlady informed her that she would have to have an extra five dollars a month since I was boarding with her.

"But I don't see what difference that makes," Winetta insisted.

"Well, there is the wear and tear on the house and the extra water." I wondered why she did not suggest the extra light. I wondered too, just what I would do to a house to cause wear and tear. Why I did not pay the five dollars, I do not know. I had a feeling that I wanted to get away from the place as quickly as possible. Again, I was blessed in finding Miss Lucy Matthews, who had a pleasant upstairs apartment with plenty of light and air. Added to that, Miss Matthews was well-educated. She enjoyed good books and often in the evenings she read to me until her voice would give out.

"I should think Miss Brown would be a lot of bother," a friend once said to Miss Matthews.

"Bother! She's no bother; she is the least trouble of anyone I ever had stay with me."

I boarded with Miss Matthews the winter following my illness at Columbia. Her home was quiet; we kept regular hours, and it was exactly what I needed. But after two years, I decided to make a change. Cuma, one of my classmates at the School for Blind, was boarding in Dayton. We thought it would be fun to be together. Our landlady was very kind and seemed not to mind any extra trouble we might cause. But there were drawbacks over which we had no control. After dinner we used to sit in the living room and visit before going to our rooms. I could hear the silver rattling on the table. "Buster," the landlady would call, and then we would hear a heavy body drop to the floor confirming our suspicions that the cat was exploring the table.

The steps in front of the house were slanting and irregular.

In the winter when they were covered with ice, they became dangerous. The landlady was not able to take care of them and yet they presented a problem for my guide and me.

Winetta took another apartment in the fall and I moved in with her again. She and her husband did not have an extra room, so we fixed up the porch swing, put up a shade for privacy, and I slept out-of-doors. I told myself it would be good for me, but sometimes when I went to bed my covers were like ice. When I awoke in the morning, there was often snow on the foot of my bed.

My next landlady lived near the school. She was kind, fat, and asthmatic. We had one thing in common—we both liked dogs. All day my landlady stayed alone, wanting somebody to talk to and not well enough to keep busy. All day I was kept working at my job, and when I returned home I wanted more than anything to be alone and have a chance to rest. After I had asked for my mail and had been civilly courteous, I would hurry to my room, throwing myself on the bed to get a few moments of relaxation before dinner. Scarcely had I made myself comfortable, when there would come a rap at the door. There would be my landlady with a piece of candy or a choice bit of gossip to furnish an excuse for her intrusion. I used to feel sorry for her and yet I grew to know what a precious thing is solitude. Inside of me there accumulated all of the unsatisfactory features of rooming and boarding with other people. They grew and were intensified until it seemed I could stand it no longer. Once I even contemplated buying a house, and visited a real estate agent for that purpose. Fortunately, I did not buy.

"Why don't you get an apartment?" Mrs. Pratt suggested, one summer while I was in Colorado. "You can buy your furniture a little at a time, and I can make your linens for you." So the next year flew by with the joy of selecting tablecloths and napkins, watching advertisements for sales on sheets and blankets, and choosing the furniture I wanted. I knew fairly well the kinds of furnishings I preferred. One of my tablecloths was to be plain with two satin strips near the edge; another was to be hemstitched and have lilies-of-the-valley all over it. My dishes were to be white with gold bands. I know of no better way to find happiness than to start working on something you've dreamed about for a long time.

I wanted a dropleaf table, which could be opened out and extended with boards, but which would occupy a very small space when closed. For my linens, I bought an old-fashioned chest of drawers. It was an antique, more than a hundred years old.

In the fall, when I had rented a three room apartment—living room, bedroom, and a large kitchen—I brought together the furniture and linens I had collected. In my bedroom there were twin Jenny Lind beds with my radio between. With twin beds I could have a friend come to visit me and I would not need to ask my landlady. There was also a dresser, two of my dining room chairs, and a little rocker like the one my mother had when I was a child, just the right size for sewing and rocking babies. In my living room was a three piece mohair suit and my music cabinet, above which was an oval mirror in a plain ma-hogany frame. On the wall opposite the mirror hung my colonial clock.

Winetta and Mary Westfall, the girl with whom I had worked at the box factory, came to help me unpack and get straightened up. Everything was new. My linens were beautifully made and my furniture had been carefully selected. I was proud of the result. It seemed I had found the solution to my problem of a place to live.

Monday evening after school I came home to an empty house. Since this was to be my first experience at cooking for myself, I decided to begin with something simple but nourishing. I would have spaghetti for supper. I boiled the spaghetti in the bottom of my double boiler, so that when I was ready to pour off the water, the lid would fit tight and I need not be afraid of getting burned. Then I browned the hamburger in a skillet. I could tell by the sound when it was brown. When it was finished, I poured in a can of tomato sauce. I spread the spaghetti into a baking dish, poured over it the contents of the skillet, tucked it in the oven and rested until it was finished. I did not seem to mind eating my supper alone. It tasted good, and having been with children all day it was a relief to sit with only my thoughts for company. Washing the dishes was easy for I was an old hand at that. I had made a beginning, and this was home.

On school days I always tried to choose dishes that were easy to fix, oven meals or boiled dinners, and often I cooked enough for more than one meal. Some of my recipes were in Braille; others I could remember from school.

I provided myself with as many little gadgets as I could find. My measuring cups were marked with raised lines on the inside, and I had five different sizes of measuring spoons. When I bought my canned goods, I tried to select the brand that had the letters raised on the label. There are hundreds of ways to make housekeeping easy for a blind person, and I tried to avail myself of them.

Once a week my sister and her husband came for supper. They always arrived after work, so I had to have the meal almost ready.

"I never believed you could keep house like this," Katherine said.

"I don't see why not. Mamma was a good housekeeper and you are too, so why shouldn't I be? I have to have everything in its place, however, in order to save time."

Sometimes in the evening when I felt particularly ambitious, I used to stir up a cake. I am especially fond of warm cake. I remember taking one out of the oven just when some of my blind friends walked in. In minutes there was nothing left but the crumbs that had been dropped. Often I invited five or six of my friends to come for the week end. We had plenty of good food to eat and we spent the rest of the time singing and playing games. One of our favorite games was hide and seek. It is more fun playing hide and seek when everyone is blind.

One of the things I had always wanted was a player piano. I bought a small studio model and a number of piano rolls. In that way I could accompany myself and sing even though I really could not play. Among my favorites were *Charmaine*, *Nola*, and *Oh, Dry Those Tears*. We spent many enjoyable

111

evenings playing and singing together these and other popular songs of the twenties.

One of the first guests who came to visit me was Mrs. Chapin. She was proud of my house and the way I kept it. She stayed for three days and after her visit I realized that there was something lacking. I could not always entertain, and so I was lonely at times. A home of my own was better than boarding, but I felt that it was only a shadow of the real thing.

After two years of living by myself, I decided to take a high school girl to stay with me. Jean was sweet and conscientious and I believe she learned quite a bit about housekeeping. But, naturally, she objected to being kept in on school nights and I decided that I had enough responsibility at school.

While Jean was with me, I went to visit a dog kennel, and brought home a cream-colored chow which she named Bruin. After school I would let Bruin out for his exercise which consisted of a two hour run by the river. His presence helped to give me the companionship I needed.

Mrs. Barney was the guest whose coming pleased me most.

"You have used good judgment, Eleanor," Mrs. Barney said, as she went from room to room, "but I think you have been rather extravagant."

"It's probably the only home I will ever make for myself and I want it nice. I spend a good deal of money trying to keep happy, but I get pretty lonesome sometimes."

"Happiness must come from within," Mrs. Barney suggested, and I realized she knew, for Mr. Barney had died and she was alone.

"There is just one disadvantage to having a home of your own. You are tied down and you can't travel very much or go to school." I had forgotten about going to school, but Mrs. Barney had reminded me and I could feel the idea beginning to grow. Suddenly all the things which I had treasured, the lovely furniture, the exquisite linens, the soft woolly blankets, the sweet-toned player piano, lost their attraction for me. Only Bruin seemed to matter, but I was dreaming again. I was charting a new course and nothing could stand in my way.

CHAPTER SEVENTEEN

At the Foot of Parnassus

It was May of 1929 when Mrs. Barney returned to Dayton. She had been in Europe for a number of years (it had seemed ages to me), and now as I sent her a bunch of lilies-of-the-valley and this greeting, my own doggerel, I realized how much I had missed her.

> Have you ever known a joy so deep
> It almost made you sad?
> Or wished for something you might do
> To show that you are glad?
> Then you will know just what I feel
> On seeing you today
> I've missed you all the dark years through
> You've been so long away.

During the ensuing summer, however, I made up for my loss. Every morning I went over to the Biltmore Hotel and spent a couple of hours with Mrs. Barney. There was seldom anything to interfere. I had been feeling the need for change, and I was eager to find out from her what that change should be.

I had learned from experience that by going on an orange juice diet for three days I was able to think more clearly, and usually something worth while came as a result. This time my inspiration was a Ph.D. I wrote my plan to Mrs. Barney in a letter one evening. The next morning she told me her plan. They were identical. I thought she had read my letter, but I discovered later that she had not yet received it.

At first, Mrs. Barney wanted me to get my Ph.D. from a European university but I decided against that. Getting a Doctor's degree is hard enough in English without having to battle with a foreign language. It seemed natural for me to decide upon Columbia University. I was familiar with it, Columbia is one of the outstanding universities in the country, and I felt I could not do better.

"I think," Mrs. Barney suggested, "it would be a good idea to take a two-year leave of absence. Do all you can at Columbia, and end up in Europe where you can continue writing your dissertation."

"What will I do with my furniture and apartment?" Suddenly, each of the things I had cherished—my linens, my kitchen cabinet, my serving table, and my china closet—had become a white elephant. Mrs. Barney had stored her furniture and now after nine years she was selling it. Little wonder then that she exclaimed, "Don't store anything. Sell everything you can. You won't get anything for it, but you'll take less if you wait." So I spent my afternoons getting rid of the treasures I had collected during my homing. I believe I minded giving up my player piano most.

That was the end of my home of my own. When I again settled down it was to the convenience of hotel life. In 1933, March first, four days before Roosevelt became president, I moved into the Dayton Biltmore Hotel. The fact that I have lived here ever since is ample demonstration that it is very satisfactory.

Having made my reservation at Columbia, and having secured my leave of absence from the superintendent, I gave up my apartment and spent the last ten days with Winetta. She had consented to keep Bruin, my cream-colored Chow. Bruin was my only regret. I can still see him sitting in the middle of the room when I was ready to depart. I knelt down beside him and put my arms around him. "I'll come back, Bruin," I promised. And I really thought I would, but for Bruin words did not suffice. He sat in his dignity, coldly aloof. He was still sitting there when I closed the door.

The day of my return to Columbia was a busy one. I was ushered into the office of Eliza Butler, the housemother of Johnson Hall.

"I understand," Miss Butler announced, "that you are planning to get a Ph.D.; that is quite an undertaking." I noticed that her speech was precise and laconic. I sensed that she had very definite ideas. "Have you made any plans as to how you are going to get along?"

"If I had a guide for a day or so here in the dormitory, it would help me to learn the lay of the land. I have attended Columbia before, and most of the buildings are not new to me." Miss Butler promised to find someone to assist me, but by the time she got around to it I had learned my way about.

As soon as I was established in my room on the sixth floor, I found someone to go over to Philosophy Hall with me. I knew that building, for I had done most of my Master's work there. I also remembered some of the professors, though I discovered that Brander Matthews had died and that John Erskine was at the Julliard School of Music. However, Ashley H. Thorndike and G. P. Krappe were still in the English department. I had decided to take my Ph.D. in English, because it would help me with my history, my writing and lecturing, and because it might lead eventually to a different position. Professor Thorndike was then the head of the English department. I had taken a course in Shakespeare under him while working for my M.A. and he remembered me when I was ushered into his office.

"I have decided to get a Ph.D.," I announced without any introduction.

"Well, if you want to get a Ph.D., I see no reason why you should not be given a chance." It was good to have his approval. During the months that followed, while others were doubting, I could always turn to his approbation and find in it the strength to go on. If he ever doubted the outcome, he never gave the slightest sign.

Alice, one of my readers, once said, "Professor Thorndike has a poker face, then suddenly it lights up. If he ever smiled at me the way he smiles at you, I don't know what I'd do. I only wish you could see him."

"Professor Patterson is our Milton instructor," Professor Thorndike explained. "I think you will like studying under him." I believe Professor Thorndike thought that since Frank A. Patterson was interested in blind Milton, he might be more willing to work with me.

That first day I talked with Professor H. M. Ayers. He was head of the Anglo-Saxon department.

"I plan to work here until I have passed my orals," I informed him, "and then go to Europe and write my dissertation there. I have a two-year leave of absence and I must have my work completed within that time."

"My advice to you," Professor Ayers said, "would be to go abroad now, forget about your Ph.D., and then go back to your teaching." Professor Ayers' manner was courteous and kind, so I did not object when he opposed my undertaking. I read and translated from the *Aeneid* and he became interested in me. It was in Anglo-Saxon, however, one of my minor fields, that I gained his confidence. I had to copy the Anglo-Saxon down and then translate from my paper. One day after I had read aloud and translated, he told a friend of mine after class that I was a remarkable woman. I was so happy that I cried.

No one knows exactly how Anglo-Saxon was pronounced, but Professor Ayers was considered a master in reading the language. I sat spellbound as I listened to him reading from the *Four Gospels*. It is one of the treasured experiences of my life.

My other minor fields were the Romantic Period, under Professor Lawrence, and the Eighteenth Century, under Professor E. H. Wright. If they had doubts as to my undertaking, they kept them to themselves. When I took my examination in German from Professor Lawrence, he said he could tell from my pronunciation that I had been well grounded in that subject. I read to him from *Die Jungfrau von Orleans*.

My language requirement in French necessitated more study. I got out my "Fraser and Squair," and boned for several weeks. I read a number of books in Braille, and then made an appointment with Professor Wright. Instead of asking me to read, he began talking to me in French. I had no difficulty in understanding and answering him, as I was used to having French read to me. That was the easiest examination I ever took, and when I thought of the weeks I had studied, I laughed.

With my language requirements out of the way, I turned my attention to the four fields I had selected. It was in my major field where trouble developed almost immediately. At first Professor Patterson was friendly enough, but suddenly I detected a change in his manner. Perhaps he expected me to fail and thought that the failure would reflect on him. He had no way of judging my capabilities at that time, for I was merely attending lectures with the rest of the students. His antagonism was quite apparent and I believe he felt he was justified in opposing my plan for a Ph.D. That antagonism, though it caused me a great deal of heartache, assured my success.

Since the time of my sojourn at Columbia was limited, I decided to do two things: to set the date for my orals for October of the following year, and to choose the subject for my dissertation as soon as possible, so that while preparing for my orals, I could gather any materials I came across for that subject.

In the seminar, Professor Patterson suggested a number of topics for dissertations, but whenever I inquired about one of them I met with a rebuff. There should be, I told myself, some subject in which I would be interested, and so I prayed for guidance. One day it came to me just as if God had spoken: "Milton's Blindess." No one who really knew about blindness had written on that subject. I could bring to it my own feelings and experiences, and I knew instantly that it would be my dissertation. I drew an outline of what I planned to do, and showed it to Professor Krappe. I had studied under him in 1919, and he was still interested in me.

"Do you think this would make a subject for a dissertation?" I asked, handing him my outline.

"I don't see why not. You have as much as anyone else to start with." His encouraging words sent me posthaste to my adviser. Professor Thorndike studied my outline carefully.

"I believe you have something," he said, and I knew he smiled as he sometimes did. "Have you shown it to Professor Patterson?"

"No, I wanted you to see it first."

"Well, show it to him and go ahead with it." I waited until

after seminar to speak to Professor Patterson.

"I believe I have found my dissertation subject."

"Well, what is it?" he asked dryly.

"Milton's blindness! No one who really knows blindness has ever written about it."

"There is nothing left to be done on Milton. I made that clear before," he snapped.

"Professor Thorndike thought I had a subject, and told me to show you my outline."

"He told you to show me this?" Professor Patterson hurried from the room; whether or not he saw Professor Thorndike, I do not know, but he returned a few minutes later, saying merely, "Go ahead and see what you can do with it."

For many years, when I had hit upon the right idea or the right plan, I knew it immediately and I never questioned the decision. So it was with my dissertation on Milton's blindness. When the book was finally completed, it followed closely my original plan; however, Professor Patterson's acquiescence had its price. From then on he scarcely spoke to me, and when he did it was to condemn my undertaking. One morning I went to ask him a question. Without answering it, he began a forceful attack upon my plan for a Ph.D. I do not recall what he said. Afterwards, his secretary, who became my friend, said, "Professor Patterson is a kind man and I have never heard him talk to anyone as he did to you today. I do not understand why." I did not understand either, but I gathered that maybe he felt he was being imposed upon by the head of the department, or that my possible failure would reflect on him.

Elizabeth Hall, who was also working for her Ph.D. and was wise in the ways of universities, advised me to go to Harvard, but I had decided upon a Ph.D. from Columbia, and from the department of which Professor Thorndike was the head. I did contemplate, however, changing my major field, so I went to talk with Professor Thorndike about it. As I sat waiting my turn in the outer office, Professor Patterson came in.

"Are you waiting to see Professor Thorndike?" he inquired.

"Yes, sir," I replied.

"A number of the professors doubt your ability to get a Ph.D. There are some things blind people can't do," he said emphatically.

"I know that too well, but getting a Ph.D. is not one of them. I would not attempt to fly an airplane, but I know my own capabilities." Professor Patterson's words stung me, and yet I felt if he had been able to get a Ph.D., I, with my extra memory training, could get one too. I am sure that he thought he was doing the right thing for me.

In Professor Thorndike's office, I repeated my conversation with Professor Patterson. Then I suggested changing my major field. I really did not want to change, because I knew that Milton's blindness was my dissertation subject, and the dissertation must be taken from the major field.

"No, I wouldn't change," Professor Thorndike advised. "I'd go ahead and work and stay away from Professor Patterson for awhile. In the summer when you have something written, send it to me and I will criticize it for you." That night before I went to bed, I thanked God that there was a man with the vision and understanding who would help me find my way to the top of Parnassus.

While I was trying to work out my problem with Professor Patterson, I was facing other difficulties. Alone they would have been surmountable, but combined they proved too much for my endurance. First, in the dormitory, life was very much restricted. There were no radios, no victrolas, and the piano was seldom heard. The absence of a radio worked a real hardship upon me. I was almost completely cut off from the outside world.

In October of 1929 Mrs. Barney came to New York. I met her in the Library at Fifth Avenue and Forty-second Street in the Department for the Blind. We went off in a corner to talk, and I sensed that something was wrong, but I did not know what it was. I suppose Mrs. Barney thought I knew about the stock market crash, so she did not bother to mention it. However, she discussed the advisability of my returning to Dayton.

"I secured a leave of absence in order to get my Ph.D.," I told her. "I am going to stay here and work until my money runs out; then I will go home to teach awhile and return to finish." This time Mrs. Barney did not try to dissuade me. Perhaps she realized that my mind was made up, or maybe she thought I did not understand the seriousness of the stock market crash. I didn't. I didn't even know there had been one. But the fact that she had wanted me to return home made me wonder if she too was questioning my ability, and the wisdom of getting a Ph.D.

At first Miss Butler, the housemother, seemed to be interested in me, but I felt repressed in her presence and living on the same floor with her did not help the matter. Something happened, however, which aroused her displeasure and helped to make my year at Johnson Hall difficult. The Van Cleves were still in New York. They were interested in my Ph.D., but I think they thought I was foolish to waste all my savings on it.

As soon as I was settled at Johnson Hall, I went to Sunday dinner with them. It was good to be together again, and be bound by the interest of another undertaking.

"Eleanor, do you prefer white or dark meat?" Mr. Van Cleve inquired jovially.

"I can't tell the difference," I laughed.

"What, you can't tell white meat from dark? I don't believe that."

"I'll bet you couldn't tell it either if you couldn't see it." Mr. Van Cleve was definitely not convinced. We had such a happy day together that the mishap which came at its close was unexpected. At Johnson Hall, the chauffeur parked the car in front of the dormitory while Mrs. Van Cleve took me inside. A few minutes after Mrs. Van Cleve left, there was a rap on my door. I opened it to find Miss Butler waiting there.

"Have you been away?" she asked casually, yet I could sense irritation in her manner.

"Yes."

"Did your friends have a chauffeur?"

"That was Mrs. Van Cleve, from the New York City School for Blind. She brought me inside."

"The chauffeur was very rude to me," Miss Butler said. "You have been told not to park in front of the entrance. I hope you will tell your friends how rude he was."

"It may be a long time before I see the Van Cleves again. I'm sorry there was a misunderstanding about the proper place to park."

Perhaps the constraint that developed out of this incident was increased in my mind. As the months passed, however, I felt more and more the restrictions of Johnson Hall. There was one bright spot, however, when Nicholas Murray Butler came to the dormitory to make his annual visit.

"I understand you are getting a Ph.D.," he said, taking my hand. "I take off my hat to you." I glowed under his praise, but the clouds were gathering, and only a little more was needed to produce a storm. Disaster came in the form of a letter from Winetta. "Bruin is missing," she wrote, and that was the straw that broke the camel's back. For a month school children, mailmen, and newsboys searched for Bruin and we ran ads in all the papers. One day in January some of the boys found his body, lying in the snow beside the river where he had played.

This news sent me up to the infirmary, and though I seemed to have only the "flu" at first, the trouble cleared up slowly. Sometimes I attended classes, and sometimes I read, but the months dragged by, and I made little progress.

Professor Patterson, however, seemed glad when I returned to class.

In the spring I requested a reservation at Johnson Hall for summer school, but Miss Butler refused because she thought I was not able to continue my work. In May I went to New Jersey for a month, reading every day while I was there; and in June I took up my residence at King's Crown Hotel. All summer I read and studied in preparation for my orals. October was rapidly approaching, and I could not afford to fail.

CHAPTER EIGHTEEN

The Hurdle

In studying for orals, you never know when you have finished. The truth of the matter is, you never are finished. You just read and read until the fatal hour and then you take your chances. The reason for this is that you couldn't possibly cover everything that has been written in the four fields. How far short of the reading goal I came I will never know. For the Seventeenth Century, Professor Patterson supplied a list which was fairly adequate.

"Since you're writing about Milton, there won't be a single question on Milton in your orals. They save that for the defense of your dissertation," Elizabeth Hall commented. I wanted to follow her advice; I felt sure she was right but I was afraid to take a chance, so I read Milton's works thoroughly three times, no small chore. I knew that every waking moment possible had to be spent in preparation, but I made a rule never to study after eleven at night. If study was important, rest was equally so. I tried to take walks out of doors whenever possible. Sometimes we read in Morningside Park. Speed in reading was essential, and I had one Spanish girl who could cover fifty pages an hour. Of course when notes were necessary the procedure was slower.

In June of 1930 I took my reading list to Professor Patterson.

"Do you think I am reading enough?" I asked him. He looked at my checked references.

"It isn't how much you read, but how much you will remember when you come up for your orals," he said jokingly.

I laughed. "I guess we'll have to wait to find that out in October, but I have had to depend on my memory a great deal, so I think I can manage."

That was the only time I saw Professor Patterson until I reminded him of my examination, a week before its occurrence. I employed, in addition to my regular readers, a couple of tutors who had already passed their orals and knew the ropes.

In the Eighteenth Century Literature class, Miss Dahl sat behind me. I did not know then that she was almost blind. I did know, however, that she had poor vision and that she stayed up every night until four A.M.

"You can't afford to do that," I warned her, "for you won't be able to stand your orals when you come up for them." One day in the spring, Miss Dahl was missing from the class. Someone told me that she had failed her orals. Her failure, however, did not make me afraid. In an emergency some people go to pieces; others wait until the emergency is past. I believed I could keep my wits about me until the ordeal was over.

Tuesday was the appointed day for Ph.D. examinations. A week before the date set for mine, Kathryn Blair, who was living at Johnson Hall, came up for hers.

"Have you heard the news?" Elizabeth asked, as she came to give me some instruction I sorely needed.

"No, what?"

"Kathryn Blair failed her orals."

"Oh, no! What happened?"

"Well, you know Kathryn is only twenty-five, and everybody thought she was too young for such an ordeal. I guess, from what I hear, she became confused and couldn't think of anything. I hope you aren't going to do that."

"I can't afford to. I haven't the time or money to come up again. What are they going to do about Kathryn?"

"She's in the infirmary at Johnson Hall now, and I think she is going away, to come back later." I could not get Kathryn off my mind, but I could not allow her misfortune to influence my examination. I found time, however, to take her a jar of jam my sister had sent me. She seemed calm and composed; I would have been crushed. Miss Anderson and Miss Burnside, the nurses who had taken care of me the spring before, were on duty in the infirmary.

"Well, it won't be long 'til you have your turn," Miss Burnside said jokingly, "and I don't want to catch you failing and coming here."

"You won't," I promised.

Miss Anderson had always been interested in my project. Every evening when she was off duty, she went with me for a walk to the little Church on Morningside Drive. There we stood together silently praying for my success.

There are many things to think of before coming up for your orals. There is even the consideration of clothes.

"Everyone," Elizabeth had said, "wears a dark suit of some kind, and above all, gloves." Mrs. Barney had given me a dark blue ensemble. The inside lining of the coat, and the dress, were striped with white. I was to wear a little black hat, black shoes, and black gloves.

Whether it is best to study until the last minute, or to do no studying the day of the examination, rests with the individual. I worked until two-thirty of October the thirteenth, and then I closed my books. I had done the best I could, and I was ready to take the consequences. I believed they would be satisfactory.

I went directly to Johnson Hall and to the infirmary.

"Oh, you look so pretty," Miss Anderson exclaimed. "You ought to feel fine." My "keyed up" nerves gave way, and I cried a little.

"Now you're all set for the examination," Miss Anderson laughed. "We'll have a cup of good strong coffee, and in three hours it will be over."

I went early to Philosophy Hall, so that I would not feel rushed. Miss Carey, Professor Thorndike's secretary, greeted me. "You don't seem nervous," she commented.

"Well, I had a little cry and a cup of strong coffee, and I think I'll do. Is Professor Thorndike going to be in on the examination?"

"Yes, he said he was going to stay. He hasn't been a bit well, but he knows you want him to be present."

"Nothing else matters, really. If he's there, I know I'll get along all right. I wonder if I may have a book to hold. It will give me something to have in my hands, in case I go blank at the beginning." Miss Carey gave me a copy of *Hamlet*, but even if I could have seen, *Hamlet* would have been no good to me, as Shakespeare did not belong in my fields.

When someone came and escorted me into the inner office, I thought Professor Thorndike was present. When I discovered that he was not, my examination had begun and I was already holding my own. That was one time when the absence of sight proved a blessing. There were seven professors lined up in a semi-circle in front of me. I was certainly in the arena. I sat in a low, upholstered chair, not the same chair, but the same place I always sat when I conferred with Professor Thorndyke. I looked around and tried to locate him. For a few minutes we talked of silly "nothings." Finally, Professor Wright said, "Well, gentlemen, it is four o'clock, and we may as well begin."

I held the copy of *Hamlet* in my hands, idly turning the pages as Professor Patterson began a period of questioning which lasted at least an hour. When I heard the first question, my mind seemed to go blank and no sound came from my lips.

"If I can only get started," I told myself, "I'll be all right." Then I began answering. Perhaps my voice trembled a little in the beginning, but it grew steady in a few minutes.

"It ought to be easier for me to take an oral examination than most people," I thought.

In the interval, time seemed as nothing; the whole world appeared at a standstill as I sat and faced the group. I quickly realized that Elizabeth Hall was again right. "As soon as they discover you know a subject, they change it. They are not eager to find out how much you know, but how much you don't know," she had said.

"Who were some of the philosophers of the Seventeenth Century?" Professor Patterson continued. I named Hobbes and Locke, but he seemed waiting for someone else. Suddenly, another voice was addressing me. It was like a strain of music, which seemed to lift me up and pull me together. It was the voice of the man who had helped me with my Master's thesis.

"Do you know a philosopher who wasn't English?" Professor Wells asked.

"Descartes," I answered without hesitation.

Professor Patterson continued the interrogation. Finally he said he had finished, and I was turned over to the tender mercies of Professor Ayres. He was kind and helpful. He did not try to confuse me, and I do not believe he questioned me very long.

When Professor Lawrence began the attack, questioning me about the literature of the Romance Period, I think I did fairly well. I had read everything we had discussed in class, for unless you have read the books themselves, it is difficult to remember rhythm, stanzaic form, style, etc.

I was glad that Professor Krappe was present even though I had not chosen his field, for I knew he was eager for me to succeed. A barrage of questions for a couple of hours leaves the brain numb, if not almost dead. When Professor Wright and the Eighteenth Century took over, I did not know as much as I hoped I would. I guess, however, that was to be expected.

"Well, gentlemen," Professor Wright said finally, "I believe that is all. You may wait in the outer office," he said to me, as he rose and came over to escort me to the door. But when I tried to stand I was unable to do so, it seemed to me that every part of my body had to be reassembled. Finally, Professor Wright helped me to my feet. In the outer office Miss Carey was waiting.

"I know you're glad that's over," she said cordially. "It won't be long now until you know."

"The longer the door remains closed," Elizabeth Hall had said, "and the more discussion, the bigger the question of your passing." So the two minutes seemed ages to me as I sat tensely erect, listening for the door to open. Finally, it did open, and Professor Wright came toward me saying,

"Allow me to congratulate you. You have done an admirable piece of work, and you have matriculated for a Ph.D."

I managed to say "Thank you," and because I began crying I started to rush out of the room. I became confused and ran into the table, but as Professor Wright took my arm and led me into the corridor, Miss Carey was calling Professor Thorndike to tell him the news.

126

"Professor Thorndike is so glad," she said, running after me. "We're all glad."

Even the woman on the elevator congratulated me, and Mrs. Haskell, the Dean of the Graduate School, and some of the girls were waiting for me downstairs. Afterwards, Mrs. Haskell told me: "Professor Patterson said you did a splendid job; that you had a marvelous memory."

To me, however, he remarked, "You did as well as could be expected, but it doesn't follow that you can do the research on a dissertation." Nevertheless, I had not failed, and the other professors were saying favorable things about my examination. At dinner that evening, Professor Thorndike told the head of the medical staff that I had passed a very creditable examination. The next day I received a letter from Professor Wright, reiterating his congratulations and asking me to become a member of the Graduate Club.

After my examination was over, Mr. and Mrs. Van Cleve met me as I came down the steps past the statue of Minerva.

"Well, I see congratulations are in order. I am proud of you, and I wish we had more like you." Those few words of praise from Mr. Van Cleve were like gold nuggets because he seldom offered praise. I felt a deep rush of gratitude such as I have rarely known. Mrs. Van Cleve put her arms around me.

"You look as pretty as a picture, and not a bit like someone who has just had a two-hour oral examination." I tried to persuade them to have dinner with me, but that was out of the question.

"You will scarcely be able to eat or sleep for the next few days," Mr. Van Cleve warned me, "but I think you had better try to get some rest before beginning on your dissertation."

In the evening, Miss Anderson came, and together we went to the little church on Morningside Drive.

Though my orals were behind me, I still had a tremendous task ahead. There was research to be done, a book to be written, defended, and finally published. Then and only then would I receive my degree of Doctor of Philosophy from Columbia University.

CHAPTER NINETEEN

Breaking Into Print

When I had finished my orals in October, 1930, I decided to go home for a few days to be sure I had a job, for the finances of the Dayton Board of Education were in bad shape. By the following Monday I was back in New York. The check which I had sent for from the Dayton Savings and Trust before my departure was waiting for me. The following day I took it to the University Bank for cashing, and was informed later that the Dayton Savings and Trust had failed. This was indeed a blow, but when I had sent for the check I did not have the slightest idea that I was going to be out of New York. Mrs. Barney had never thought I was practical, and with this occurrence, my reputation for carelessness was confirmed. I cared less for the money, which was later refunded, than I did about Mrs. Barney's disappointment.

With the stock market crash, the failure of the Dayton Savings and Trust, and the depression, my trip to Europe was forfeited. Everyone thought I was disappointed, but the truth was, I was glad, for I felt I needed all my time and energy for the work at hand.

While studying for my orals, I had been thinking of my dissertation and gleaning every scrap of information I came across. I prepared a synopsis of Part One to send to Professor Thorndike. After a couple of weeks, he returned it with a cheery letter, saying that the material was interesting, but needed a more complete presentation.

"I have found only a couple of medical opinions on the cause of Milton's blindness," I told Mr. Van Cleve. "I ought to have some views from doctors of today."

"I think we can manage that all right," Mr. Van Cleve said.

"I am president of the Board for the Prevention of Blindness, and I'll send letters to ten or twelve doctors, asking for their opinions." So it was that I received statements from Dr. Wilmer of Johns Hopkins Hospital, from Dr. Cutler of New York City, from Arnold Sorsby of London, from Dr. Brown of Columbus, and others. Dr. Brown had been attending opthalmologist at the School for the Blind when I was a little girl. There was also a letter from Dr. Sattler. I was greatly indebted to him, for he had put an end to my headaches and had so improved my appearance that I was able to get my position at Steele High School. I recall how radiantly happy I was when I realized that the unsightliness of my eyes no longer made me conspicuous.

With my orals completed, I devoted myself entirely to reading for my dissertation. I purchased two bibliographies on Milton, one a supplement of the other. I read books on opthalmology, syphilis, medicine, and hygiene in the Seventeenth Century, and even visited insurance companies for information on infant mortality. I employed a library student to look up references in the catalog and to make out the call slips. In the mornings and the evenings I read from the books that could be taken out. In the afternoons I went to the library with two readers, one of whom copied the material on cards while the other read to me. Had the Talking Book been available when I was working on my Ph.D., it would have saved me considerable money and time.

By February I had read everything I could find. Later, when I came back to Ohio, President Thompson secured a number of books from the Ohio State University Library. He wrote: "I remember you as a young college girl and I recall the interest that Mr. Van Cleve and I had in your progress. I am delighted that you are now approaching your Doctor's Degree and wish you every possible success." President Thompson planned to come to New York and I looked forward to seeing him again, but this trip was prevented by the illness of his daughter. He died before my book came off the press.

My health, which had been declining for a long time, was beginning to fail.

"How are you coming with your book?" Mr. Van Cleve

asked.

"I'm not," I replied dully. "I seem to be at a standstill. I have done all the reading, and now I am supposed to copy my notes in Braille, but I don't seem to have the strength or courage to do it."

"I think I can help you out," Mr. Van Cleve explained. "I'll have our librarian stereograph your notes for you. It should take about a week and then you can begin writing your book." Once again Mr. Van Cleve had aided me at a crucial time.

In writing my book I planned to dictate directly to my typist, to have it read back, then to rearrange and have it typed again. I worked all during the spring and summer, and came back to Dayton just in time to start teaching. That was in 1932, and the finances of the Board of Education were growing steadily worse. That year I believe we had about six and a half months of school. For the first two months, until after election, I taught three days a week. All of my spare time was used in rewriting my book, so that by December it was ready to be sent to the committee for approval. As soon as I dropped the package in the mail, I began waiting eagerly for its return. Just before Christmas a letter came from Professor Patterson. A letter concerning my dissertation from anyone would have been a real Christmas gift, but from him it was doubly precious. I realized then how much I had missed his valuable cooperation. The professor wrote: "I am glad to be able to write you, in time for your Christmas holiday, that the committee appointed by Professor Thorndike to pass upon your dissertation has reported favorably. Naturally, there are some revisions; there always are. It seems to me, personally, that you have done a very creditable piece of work."

It was Professor Thorndike's letter, however, that thrilled me most. It ended: "Let me congratulate you on nearing the end of a very remarkable achievement. We are all impressed by the mental concentration and energy which you have shown."

Forthwith, I mailed a scarf I had knit for Professor Thorndike and enclosed one of my poems:

I raised my eyes unto a distant hill,
For well I knew I thither needs must fare,
Fearful the steeps, yet wonderful the height,
And as I gazed Sir Galahad stood there.

Not he who sought the Holy Grail, save that
In every part the same, e'en to his smile,
O, might he stay till I essayed to climb
And rest him there, and give me strength the while.

Lo! As I prayed, he vanished from the height
Yet stood beside me in the vale below.
"Since thou wouldst climb," he said in accents calm,
"It were better that together we should go."

And if some day I gain the glorious height,
And men acclaim the laurels I have won,
I would that they might know the help he gave,
His guidance in the race that I have run.

By April, I had done all I knew how to do on *Milton's Blindness*. On Monday afternoon, Professor Thorndike wrote me that he saw no reason why I should not come up for the defense of my dissertation in May, provided I could mail the required number of copies within the week. But before Professor Thorndike's letter reached me, he had died suddenly of a heart attack. He had lived long enough to see that my degree was assured.

The defense of a dissertation is an agreeable task. "Remember," Elizabeth Hall had advised, "no one knows as much about your subject as you do." It should be a nice feeling for once at least, knowing more than the professors.

With Professor Thorndike gone, at first I dreaded my return to Columbia. It could never be the same place to me. It was Professor Patterson, however, who made my return easy.

"I wish to assure you that you will have no unusual difficulties with the examination. Everyone is agreeably disposed toward you, and you have nothing to fear. Though I conscientiously opposed your attempting to write a dissertation in the first place, since you passed the matriculation examinations in a very creditable manner I have felt entirely different toward the subject."

On Tuesday of the week of May twenty-fifth, I left for New York. It was much the same as I remembered it. The flower man still stood on the corner of 116th Street, selling roses and carnations. The organ grinder with his monkey played beneath my window.

This time we met in the Library—fifteen professors and myself. We sat around a long table as they questioned me, and I felt happy and at ease. I do not recall much of what was said, and it did not seem to me that the defense lasted very long. Then everyone congratulated me and I hurried back to Dayton to finish the last week of school. Yet I knew that until I published my dissertation, my degree would not be forthcoming.

Mr. Van Cleve promised to see about the editing of my book, as it would be more convenient for someone in New York to look after the job. The publication would cost me more than eight hundred dollars, so in order to finance the book we planned to sell autographed copies ahead of time, which would lessen the debt. The question of size, binding, and type were left to Mr. Van Cleve. The editing was done in New York. I came in on the galley proof, the final proof, and, though I hadn't planned it, the writing of the blurbs.

I went to the Chapins for the weekend. There I talked with Edward S. Parsons, president of Marietta College, who was a Milton scholar, and his help and inspiration were invaluable in the preparation of the book. Later, I settled down to listen to Mr. Chapin read aloud every word I had written. By the time we had finished we were both too tired to think of the blurbs. The galley proof had to be returned to New York by Sunday evening, so I spent that day saying nice things about my own book. A letter from Mr. Van Cleve stated: "Mr. Chapin did a splendid job with the galley proof, but he was especially fine on the blurbs. They ought to help sell the book!"

Suspense is wonderful, but wearing. Sometimes I thought I could not wait until my first book was in my hands. The suspense, however, was culminated early in April of 1934.

Milton's Blindness is a beautiful book. I refer to its trappings, not to the contents. The binding is dark red, with an open book on the cover, in which is written Columbia University Press. At the top of the open book is the King's Crown, because in the early years Columbia University was known as King's College.

The book is dedicated to Elinore M. Barney. Someone once asked Kingsley what was the secret of his strong, joyous life, and he answered, "I had a friend."

In the preface I wrote:

> Blindness came upon Milton in adult life, but it has been a part of my life as far back as I can remember. . . . To the interpretation of Milton's life and writings after the loss of sight, I add my knowledge of blindess; and on account of this bond of union, I bring to the task an interest such as Milton must have given to the writing of *Samson Agonistes*.

The book contains four parts; the first part deals with the cause of Milton's blindness, and the first chapter is "Medicine and Hygiene in the Seventeenth Century." Over this first chapter there was considerable discussion. Professors Krappe and Thorndike thought it should be included, but Professor Patterson was sure it had no place in a book on Milton. The first chapter furnishes, I believe, the background for the rest of the section. With it, you may understand the scientific advancement, and the gross medical ignorance of the seventeenth century, which make a decision as to the cause of Milton's blindness impossible. Part Two is "Autobiographical References to His Blindness"; Part Three, "Milton, as Reflected in His Poetry"; Part Four, "Milton's Eyes Take Holiday."

The style of *Milton's Blindness* is simple and more readable than that of most dissertations, but since it is not the kind of book the general public reads, its sale has been limited.

The first autographed copy went to Mrs. Barney, the second to Franklin Delano Roosevelt, and the third to Mr. and Mrs. Van Cleve.

Requirements having been duly fulfilled, I was to receive my degree in June, 1934. I had never owned a cap and gown, but now that I was to have a Ph.D. degree I thought I would indulge. Mr. Chapin and President Parsons ordered it through Marietta College.

At Steele, each day at noon one of the boys went for my mail. One day he came back lugging a suit box. My curiosity was keen and my students seemed eager, too, as we opened the box then and there. Excitement ran high when they saw the cap and gown and we spent the next five minutes of class time learning how it was supposed to be worn. It was heavy black silk trimmed with dark blue velvet bands on the sleeves and down the front. The inside lining of the hood was white, and a gold tassel on the mortar board, a gift from the Chapins, completed the whole. If my boys and girls had all been working for Ph.D.'s they could not have been more enthusiastic. When again I left for New York in June of 1934, I carried with me a purse from the class that had shared so completely in my success.

At commencement, suddenly the band began playing, the cameras grinding, and we walked slowly toward the platform with the statue of Minerva looking down upon us. We crossed High Street, marching through a double line of professors, and took our places on chairs upon the steps. This was the moment for which I had waited, for which I had worked and prayed. Perhaps I was too excited to hear much that the speakers said. Perhaps I was too confused by the many microphones to know just where the speaker's stand was located. When we took our seats the sun was warm and bright. Finally the clock chimed six and commencement was over. The sun had disappeared behind the tall buildings of New York City, and I, who had worked for four years on the consummation of a Ph.D., stood a little bewildered now that it was finished.

In my purse was a letter from Nicholas Murray Butler. I knew what it said by heart:

> I find it difficult to express in words my appreciation of the amazing task you have completed in writing your book on Milton's blindness. Not only is it an outstanding contribution to a subject of great importance, of which the world has long been in total ignorance, but in your own case it represents a triumph not only of mind but of character which entitles you to permanent distinc-

tion and remembrance. You have been able by sheer strength of will and elevation of spirit to associate your own name with that of Milton so long as the literature of Milton remains.

With highest appreciation and congratulations without qualification of any kind, I am,

Sincerely yours,
Nicholas Murray Butler

The real surprise with reference to my teaching came when Mr. Holmes, my principal, and Frances Brown, editor of the *Steele Lion*, decided to print an issue in my honor. It contained a picture of me in my cap and gown, and articles by teachers and former students of Steele.

I received letters from Mrs. Roosevelt, Harry Jeffrey, who later became a congressman, D. S. Wood (from Capetown, South Africa), B. A. Wright (from the University of Glasgow), and my old friends Nina Rhodes and Georgia Trader. There was even a letter from Professor Denis Saurat, whose theory that Milton's blindness was the result of congenital syphilis I had cruelly attacked in my book.

There were reviews of my book in *The Medical Review of Reviews*, the *British Medical Journal*, the *South African Medical Journal*, and the *New York Times Supplement*.

Friends and former students collected a number of newspaper articles from the *New York Herald Tribune*, the *Washington, D. C. Star*, the *Columbus Dispatch*, the *Los Angeles Express*, the *Washington Post*, the *Boston Transcript*, the *New York Telegram*, the *Los Angeles Times*, and the *Helgens Nyheter* of Stockholm.

Besides medical journals and newspapers, articles appeared in *Modern Language Notes*, *Time*, *Modern Philology*, the *London Times Literary Supplement*, *Year's Work in English Studies*, and the *South Atlantic Quarterly*.

More articles appeared in the *New Beacon*, *Sight Saving Review*, and the *Ziegler Magazine*, publications for the blind. President Parsons wrote a review which appeared in *And There Was Light*, another magazine about the blind. A more scholarly review of my book was written by S. C. Swift, the blind librarian of the Canadian National Institute, in *Outlook For the Blind*. Tireless, too, in his efforts for my success, Mr. Van Cleve wrote an article for this magazine.

There was little unfavorable criticism of the book. Perhaps scholars hesitated because of my blindness. What was said made little difference to me, because so far as I was concerned, the subject was closed. This may indicate that I am not a scholar, but when I had completed my Ph.D., I was too exhausted ever to want to continue my research on the subject of *Milton's Blindness*.

In December of 1934, Frances Jones, a former Steele student and an instructor at Ohio State University, planned that I should become an honorary member of Chi Delta Phi literary sorority. At the reception for the occasion I stood as the guest of honor in the receiving line. After dinner with the members of the National Organization, the ceremony of initiation was enacted and the pin of Chi Delta Phi was fastened to my dress.

Recognition from Ohio State University was pleasant to me. The write-up in the *Daily Ohio State Lantern* said:

> First blind student to attend Ohio State, first blind woman to receive a Doctor's degree, the only blind teacher in the Dayton Public Schools—these are a few of the distinctions attained by Eleanor G. Brown, '14.

Like the brook, news of my Ph.D. seemed to run on forever. Thanks to Frances Jones, I was written up in *American Women*. Later I was made a member of the Eugene Field Society and the Mark Twain Society and I received from the Alumni Association of the Graduate Schools of Columbia University special mention in a contest for the person "who had made a distinct contribution to the human race in any field of endeavor during the year 1934."

Still the three letters that I prized most came from Mr. Van Cleve, Harry Emerson Fosdick, and President Parsons. President Parsons' letter concluded: "I am wondering what will now be 'the fresh fields and pastures new.'"

CHAPTER TWENTY

Tramp, Tramp, Tramp

When the tumult and the shouting of my Ph.D. had died away, I felt as if I never wanted to study again, as if I would even try to forget all I had learned, and do nothing but teach and rest. There is, however, a restless self-dissatisfaction about me. I enjoy trying to fulfill a determination or searching for new adventure. Generally my strength does not keep pace with the goals for which I strive. But when I plan to hold to a normal pace, in order to build up my reserve, I am restless. I am drifting; I am in search of something, but I do not know what. I try out all the hopes and dreams which I keep in the background while I am striving for a goal. Suddenly the goal, once so distant, loses its charm with nearness, and in due time another goal appears to take its place.

I was in such a mood of unrest that I talked, one afternoon, with Mrs. George Shaw Greene and Mrs. S. S. King, whom I had known previously.

"Since you like to lecture, why don't you get a Seeing Eye dog?" Mrs. Greene asked.

"I've always thought I was conspicuous enough without a dog, and I've never been sure the Board of Education would permit me to have one. In 1929, Morris Frank, now Vice President of the Seeing Eye, had sent me a telegram: 'I have reserved a place in the September class.' I was just going to Columbia, so I wired back, 'Going to get a Ph.D.; no time for dogs.'"

"I should think you would like to have a dog," Mrs. Greene urged, and I could feel myself beginning to weaken, for I like dogs, and I wanted to give as many lectures as possible.

"The age limit is fifty, and I am already forty-nine," I

suggested.

"Suppose I write to the Seeing Eye and tell them you want to apply. Would you like me to do that?" Mrs. King questioned. I thought of my restlessness; maybe this was the way out, and so I gave my consent.

In February, Mrs. Campbell came from the Seeing Eye to visit me. She tested me on directions, my walking speed, and my ability to handle myself, then she inquired if I could keep a dog.

My application was accepted in March and I was to go for training in June. Immediately I began to prepare. I practiced walking three miles an hour, in order to get ready for the fifteen miles a day at the Seeing Eye. This strenuous exercise, after teaching, was difficult, but it was nothing in comparison to the rigors of the training at the Seeing Eye. I secured the most sensible walking shoes I could find, for high heels and Seeing Eye dogs do not mix.

The Seeing Eye is located near Morristown, New Jersey. Morristown was chosen because, as an old revolutionary town, it has only one straight street. The sidewalks are brick, cement, and board, and often a flight of steps leads to the street. If you can find your way about in Morristown, you can manage in any part of the United States.

I arrived at the Seeing Eye on Sunday, June 4th. Mr. Debetaz met me at the door, for he was to be my trainer. He is from Switzerland, and was then head trainer at the Seeing Eye. As I entered the reception hall, Mr. Debetaz dropped my arm.

"You must go here by yourself," he said in broken English. "Walk about ten feet to the stairway, at the landing, turn left; at the top of the stairs, turn right to the room at the end of the hall. You will not have a roommate for the other girl was unable to come at the last minute." In a way I was glad for this, for I was tired, school having just closed, and I wanted to be alone.

When Mr. Debetaz had gone downstairs, I explored my room. It was a large corner room, with windows on three sides, and a bath adjoining. I noticed that all the floors were covered with linoleum. I suppose, where there are so many dogs, it is

138

easier to keep clean.

At the other end of the corridor were the rooms for men, and in the middle a living room which I dubbed "No Man's Land." On the lower floor were the dining room, kitchen, and offices. The house is a large comfortable white one with green trimmings, and squarely built.

All day Sunday, as I unpacked and wrote letters, I kept listening for the dogs to bark. When would I get my dog? What would she be like? What would the training be like? These, and a dozen other questions, kept running through my mind. At six o'clock, feeding time, a hundred dogs barked for their food. They were in the kennels, behind the house.

There were three regular members of our class: Carston Ohnstead, from Minnesota, who has since published *The World at My Fingertips*, Ray McGuire, from Wichita, Kansas, and myself. Then there was a Mr. Coleman whose sojourn was brief, because the training was too strenuous for him.

The fifth member of our class, Mr. O'Neil, was working to become a trainer at the Seeing Eye. In order to receive his diploma, he was required to spend four weeks under blindfold, and to be guided by a dog. Mr. O'Neil furnished more amusement during my stay than anyone, especially at the table, where he tried in vain to cut his steak and get it safely to his mouth still blindfolded.

The sixth member of the class, Dr. Benton, an osteopath, came back to Morristown to return a dog and get another. His first dog was more interested in lady friends than he was in his master, and was sold minus his harness for a pet. I remember Dr. Benton especially because he taped my ankles, which were rebelling against the ten to fifteen mile hikes each day.

The last member of our class, and he could hardly be called of our class, was Morris Frank, there to secure Buddy II. Mr. Frank, in many ways, helped me to keep on an even keel, for he would sometimes talk to me of the loss of his first dog, and of how much my dog would mean to me.

I was the only woman in the class, and I suspect I tried Mr. Debetaz, who didn't seem to care about training women.

Yet, I had the best trainer the Seeing Eye employed and I came away with a first class dog.

On Monday our training began. Work started with a lecture by Mr. Dedetaz. We were not allowed to take notes, so usually by the time I figured out what he was saying (his English was difficult for me to understand) I forgot what he really had said. All of the men were familiar with the Seeing Eye dogs and their trappings. As for me, I was in a new world and very much adrift. Mr. Debetaz explained all the various commands. Then with him as our dog, Juno, each one of us in turn went over our first route giving such orders as "forward, Juno," "Left," "Right," "Steady," "Halt," and "Good girl." We kept the handle of the harness, which he held, clasped in our hand.

In the afternoon there was another lecture by Mr. Debetaz, but still no dog. The suspense was nerve-wracking. I wanted to see my dog more than anything in the world, to know her name, and what she looked like. But Mr. Debetaz explained it this way.

"We have to study the students, in order to decide which dog is best suited to them. What kind of dog would you rather have," he asked, "a gossipy dog or one that tends strictly to business? By a gossipy dog, I mean one that likes to pick out restaurants and candy stores and mingle with people." Of course the men wanted a dog that tended strictly to business.

"I want both!" I exclaimed.

"But you can't have both," Mr. Debetaz answered with finality, but as it turned out I got both.

Tuesday morning Mr. Humphrey, then head of the Seeing Eye, lectured. The only thing I remember that he said was, "Students with college degrees are hardest to train." Maybe that explains why I was so stupid. Tuesday morning, too, "Juno" was still going strong. I could scarcely sleep or eat thinking about my dog, but on Tuesday afternoon our meeting took place.

"Here is a nice piece of meat," Mr. Debetaz said. "Hold it in your hand, and when your dog takes it from you snap the leash onto her collar and take her to your room. Her name is Topsy, and she is a black Chesapeake Retriever." I heard the click of Topsy's nails on the linoleum floor as Mr. Debetaz led her up the stairs, across the hall, and into the living room where I sat. I was tense with expectation and eagerness. I held the meat in my hand waiting for Topsy to take it. Then I held it out to her, and she swallowed it with one gulp. I found the ring on her collar and snapped on the leash. I had always thought of Seeing Eye dogs as shepherds with long silky fur, beautifully glossy and attractive to the touch. I had never seen a dog like Topsy, and somehow I formed the opinion that she was not good-looking. Also when I first saw her, she smelled doggy. She was thin and long-legged, with webbed feet. Her coat was rough and she certainly was not pleasing to the touch. Whatever I thought she lacked in beauty, she certainly made up for in enthusiasm and devotion.

Though I was disappointed, Topsy gave no sign of being wounded. She laid her head in my lap, put her feet on the keys of my typewriter, and did everything imaginable to win my affection. When I think of my coldness to her and her eagerness to please, I am ashamed.

The following morning I learned to put on Topsy's harness, which consisted of a leather band just behind her front legs. To this girdle, on her back, a U-shaped handle bar was fastened. The girdle was kept in place at the front by a T-shaped strap. The guiding bar was metal, covered with leather. When my hand grasped it Topsy went on duty. At that moment she became a Seeing Eye dog and her responsibility showed in her changed attitude. When Topsy stepped down, the bar on her harness slanted up; when she stepped up, the bar slanted down.

Around her neck Topsy wore a link collar, with a plate at the back reading, "Seeing Eye, Morristown, New Jersey." Her leash was fastened to a ring in the chain, and when she failed to do her duty or forgot who was boss, I would jerk the leash which tightened her collar and say, "Pfui," which means "for shame!" This is the only way Seeing Eye dogs are corrected. In this way I hurt her feelings immensely, but I seldom hurt her. Sometimes when I dropped her harness in order to punish her, she would hand me her paw or lean close to me to break the force of the jerk.

141

Topsy's leash had two lengths. The shorter one was used when she was working and was held in the left hand with the harness bar. When the bar was dropped, Topsy went off duty and became, for the time at least, just a dog. The longer leash was used for heeling.

Topsy's trousers were satiny smooth and very shiny. The hair on her legs was so short that people often thought she had been clipped. But being a Chesapeake retriever, a dog that swims for ducks, Topsy needed hair that would dry quickly. The coat on her back looked like caracul, and laid in deep waves which covered her body from the crown of her head to the tip of her tail. Her coat felt like plush or velvet. Her head was satiny like her slender legs, and its beauty was enhanced by long, soft ears. Her body was heavy, with a powerful chest and broad shoulders.

On Wednesday morning I went with Mr. Debetaz to Morristown for the first excursion in the company of my dog. Perhaps I was not too steady on my feet. Surrendering to the guidance of a dog is not the easiest thing in the world. As we hurried along, a little boy, running backwards, went between my feet and I fell. I loved Topsy from that moment. I shall never forget her misery. She thought she was to blame, and licked my skinned knees, acting as if she had lost her last friend. But soon we were up and off again, and our downfall was forgotten.

Wednesday afternoon we went over a new route, and by Thursday we were ready to follow that route alone. Mr. Debetaz did not walk behind us as usual; he went through alleys, took short cuts, watching us whenever possible, whether we were conscious of it or not. I was happy to be on my own. Perhaps it was this joy or maybe it was the work of the Almighty, but when I went through traffic I knew no fear. Topsy and I were together and free. We could go wherever, whenever, and as far as we pleased.

Sometimes our class went to Morristown on the bus in order that we might have the practice of traveling with our dogs. One day as I dismounted from the bus at the Seeing Eye, Topsy's leash slipped from my grasp. Joyfully she ran up the drive to the house with Mr. Debetaz in pursuit. "Hold on to your dog,"

142

he ordered sternly when he brought her back to me. They told me afterward that had Topsy gone to the kennel instead of the house, they would have decided that she was not the dog for me. How much joy I should have missed!

Each day our walks grew longer and more difficult. A dog with four legs travels faster than a human with two. I found it hard to keep up, for Topsy and I followed the men and there was always a race.

My time at the Seeing Eye was not all spent in work. Much was made of the lunch and dinner hour. We were not allowed to talk shop, but occasionally I was so thrilled with my experience that I forgot. How could I be expected to refrain from talking about my new-found freedom after forty-nine years of dependence?

Morris Frank sat at the end of the table with his new dog Buddy II. Buddy did not fancy the cats which were kept at the school in order to teach the dogs not to chase them. When one was let into the dining room he gave vent to his disapproval by a leap and a bark. Morris paid little heed, for his thoughts were of a grave under the elms in the front yard where Buddy I lay sleeping.

Mr. Ebeling, vice president of the Seeing Eye, always had lunch with us. He was a gentleman of the old school, and I treasure his kindness and understanding more than any other memory of the Seeing Eye.

One day Alexander Woolcott came for lunch in order to see Morris Frank's new dog. He was an ardent patron of the Seeing Eye. As was his custom, he did most of the talking and we listened to catch his constant flow of humor.

Mealtime was a happy time for Topsy, too. I think she always hoped there might be a handout for her. Generally, she refused to go under the table. Perhaps she did not want to miss anything. The men's dogs were saintly and always did exactly what they were told. Sometimes there were twelve people at our table, and ten dogs under it, but there was not a dog fight while I was there.

One day Mr. Ohnstead dropped a piece of pie between his

feet. As he sat wondering what he was going to do about it, with Topsy on one side of him and his dog, Flander, on the other, Topsy reached over and with one slurp the pie was gone. Ohnstead wondered what Flander was going to do about that, but Topsy and Flander had roomed together in the kennels, and so Flander paid no heed.

The walk to the park, where we aired our dogs, was circuitous. Topsy was always eager to join the rest of her canine friends. There, we took off the harnesses and walked back and forth on the gravel, until our feet struck the grass on one side or the cement on the other. In order to keep myself company I sang as I marched, while Topsy diverted herself with a mahogany kitten. On Saturday we trained for only a half day. I was so happy that I warbled a song I had learned as a child:

Saturday has come at last—welcome day!
All the weary week has passed—welcome Saturday!

During the third week of my training, Mr. Debetaz took Topsy to be wormed. She was gone for an hour; but it seemed like a year. I can still hear her eager feet as she tore up the stairs and came back to me. I knew then how much a part of me she had become.

At the end of three weeks the men were allowed to go home. I was kept for a few more days, because I needed special training for school and because Mr. Debetaz wanted to see how Topsy would work by herself, as she had heretofore followed the other dogs. She worked fine, and before the training was over we were doing fifteen miles a day, up hill, down dale, along grassy paths and cement sidewalks, under trees with low hanging branches, in rain or shine.

In order to test the results of training, every student must make one or two trips to Newark, New Jersey. There, at five P.M. the traffic is heavier than any other place in the world. One afternoon while the rain came down in torrents, Topsy and I made our pilgrimage to Newark. Topsy always hated rain, and at every corner she tried to turn in the direction where the station wagon was parked. Finally we came to Market Street, which is exceedingly wide with a car track in the center. When I reached the middle of the street and was passing in front of a loading car, I suddenly heard the scream of a siren and the clang of a fire engine bell. I could not stand in front of a street car. I dared not retreat. I calculated the distance, and decided that I could make it to the opposite curb before the red devil passed.

"Hop up," I ordered, and Topsy sprang forward. I heard the fire engine rush by as we stepped onto the curb.

"Topsy never flinched a muscle," I said to Mr. Debetaz.

"Neither did you," he replied. That was the first word of commendation I had received. Then I knew that for Topsy and me, it would be we two together.

The fourth week of my stay at the Seeing Eye, a new class came. There were eight men and women from all parts of the United States. I could not discuss the training, nor show them my dog. A gulf lay between us, though a common interest bound us together. I was going home. They were just beginning their training. They were happy in my accomplishment, and were looking forward to their own departure. I do not recall their names, but I remember their friendliness and their cheery good-byes as I started for the station. I was eager to go home, yet, with Topsy in the kennel waiting to be shipped, my hands seemed empty, and a part of me—gone !

CHAPTER TWENTY-ONE

Topsy Goes to School

"Where's Tops?" Mrs. Greene asked when she met me at the Dayton station.

"For her first trip, she will come in a crate. She will be here Wednesday."

If Mrs. Greene was disappointed, she said nothing. She had seen Topsy at the Seeing Eye, so she could afford to wait. As for me, I saw few people, for I did not want to explain the absence of Topsy. I was feeling the separation more than I could comprehend.

"When Topsy comes to the Biltmore," Mr. Breene, the assistant manager, had said, "the hotel will feed her." Everything was in readiness long before the time of Topsy's arrival. There was a blanket for her bed, and a dish and pan for eating and drinking. The chain which was to anchor her to my bed at night was attached, though I never used it after the first week.

All day Wednesday I waited for Topsy's coming. I phoned the depot several times, but no Topsy. Finally I became desperate. Suppose they had taken her further west or put her on the wrong train? I thought of a hundred things that might have happened, and ended by telegraphing the Seeing Eye. The answer came promptly. Topsy had been crated on Monday night and someone had forgotten to ship her Tuesday. Thursday was another day of waiting. At three o'clock Mr. Carroll, the porter, announced that Topsy had arrived.

I can still hear the beat-beat of her tail against the crate as I approached to release her. She whined plaintively and sniffed. She was frantic when I took her out. She could not walk straight and jumped on me as if we had been separated for a year. She was Dayton's first Seeing Eye dog and newsmen were waiting to take her picture. She was scared, tired, and hungry; she looked thin and ill, hardly in condition to be photographed. When the newsmen had left, I fed her and sat down to assure her of no future separation.

I knew she was dirty and needed a bath, so I called Marbeth and her mother, friends of mine, and they came immediately to my rescue. In their back yard we scrubbed Topsy for the first time. She was almost too tired to play, but she rolled in the sunshine to dry herself and then lay at my feet. We sat on the lawn as evening came. I thought of the problems I might have to solve, the pitfalls that lay ahead, and the prejudice I might have to overcome. Topsy stretched full length on the cool grass. Only her head rested on my foot as if she wanted to be sure that while she slept I would not escape. She could not know that separation would be as painful to me as to her.

Ninety per cent of the Seeing Eye dogs are German Shepherds. It was natural then that people should expect to see a dog with head and ears erect, traversing the streets of Dayton. It is only within the last few years that the Seeing Eye has trained other breeds. Now the Seeing Eye uses any smart dog with two coats of hair. Topsy was chosen for her gentleness and background. She had belonged to a millionaire in Chicago and for the first year of her life had slept by the crib of a three-year-old child.

If the public was disappointed in Topsy when she first came to town, the newspapers went to considerable trouble to play her up as Dayton's first Seeing Eye dog. In the Sunday *News* there was a half-page spread with a large four-column picture of Topsy, an article, and six smaller pictures. Topsy and I, with our excursions through the streets, did the rest.

"When you get home," Mr. Debetaz had advised, "don't take your dogs downtown for a few days. Work them in your neighborhood."

In the beginning, Topsy's job was more difficult than the average Seeing Eye, for we lived at the Biltmore Hotel in the center of Dayton. If we wished to go out, even for a breath of air, we had to go through the heaviest traffic. Sometimes all the people coming toward us in the square would turn and follow us. If Topsy made a mistake she was punished in front of an audience. She made good use of this situation by dropping her head, tail, and ears, and looking as if I had half killed her. She looked soulful enough under normal conditions.

Seeing Eye dogs are not supposed to be gun shy. But the Fourth of July is a test of any dog's fortitude, and Topsy spent the day in apprehension. Her body quivered from head to foot.

It is hard to estimate how much Topsy or any other dog knows. I have seen some dogs who seem to know more than people, and I am sure Topsy thought she knew more than I did. Seeing Eye dogs are taught to obey single words such as "Forward," "Left," "Right," "Steady," and "Halt." Sometimes these commands are preceded by the dog's name. I may say, "Topsy, fetch!"

The first day Topsy was in Dayton, I decided to take her around the square. When we came out of the hotel, I said "Topsy, forward, left," and we went toward First Street. When we reached the curb I made a half turn to the left, motioned with my hand, and said, "Topsy, left, forward." As she started on First Street I sang out, "Good girl." At the entrance of the garage, Topsy looked left and right to see if any cars were coming in or out. At the alley she hesitated, but did not stop at the curb because it was low. Again she looked to right and left for cars that might cross our path. This procedure is very important, as it is not always possible to hear the cars as they creep by. In this manner we went around the square. When we reached the entrance of the hotel I did not remind Topsy to turn in. Mr. Debetaz had said, "Don't let your dog turn in the first time, for if you do, he will always want to." Well, I went around the block dozens of times, but Topsy never passed the entrance without making a desperate attempt to worm her way in. This should be a splendid advertisement for the hotel.

Our next trip was to the department store. Topsy and I started out of the hotel as usual. When we came to First Street, Topsy took me to the curb and halted. Then her head pressed

148

against my knee lest I be too near the edge of the step or the passing traffic. There was something kind and protecting in that big head against my knee.

Neither Topsy nor I could distinguish between the colors of the traffic lights. We stood on the curb and as the cars rolled by Topsy watched their movements, and I listened to the sound of their passing. "Forward," I commanded, when the traffic began to move on Main Street. Suddenly Topsy checked; a belated car which I did not hear, was slipping through the stop light. The Seeing Eye calls this refusal to go forward, when the command has been given and the path is not clear, "Legitimate disobedience." I wanted to hug Topsy then and there.

Someone told me that in crossing the street both ways, I would avoid the traffic on the near side if I always crossed to the left; so I chose to traverse First Street and then Main. On the far side of First Street, cars were coming around the corner. Topsy looked to see if they were going to stop. When they continued to move, she checked close beside them so that I might not be hit from the rear. After the cars had passed, Topsy moved forward, and as her harness sloped down, I knew we had reached the curb. We had gone through traffic for the first time in Dayton.

In the same manner we crossed Main Street and turned left toward Second. Rike-Kumler's store is situated at Second and Main, and we went there to get some dog biscuits. As we passed the front of the store, I was able to locate the entrances by means of the facial sense. At one of these I said, "Topsy, right." There are double doors leading into the store, so Topsy led me to where I might grasp the handle of the door. As we entered, a cool breeze greeted me. Topsy's nails clicked joyfully on the bare floor, and her tail wagged happily as we worked through the crowd. Her nose sniffed the candy and food, so that when I was ready to start for home, she was loath to leave.

The older Topsy and I grew, and the longer we were together, the surer I was that she thought—if by thinking one means the use of judgment. Sometimes when Topsy and I went for a walk, we were blocked by a car parked across a sidewalk.

Topsy would take me up close enough so that I could see what it was. Yet I was often unable to decide whether it was better to go to the left or to the right. So I would keep on saying "Forward." She, in turn, looked first to the right and then to the left and when she had made a decision over which I had no influence, we went around the car. When we were back on the sidewalk I would say, "Good girl. Forward!"

Ever since I was a child I have been familiar with the map of Dayton. Yet there are pitfalls of which I was unconscious until I secured Topsy. On First Street there is a grating over an opening in the center of the sidewalk. Sometimes the grating is removed. Topsy would take me up to the hole, and when I was dangerously close to the brink she swung around it. One day at Monument Avenue I commanded, "Topsy, right." She continued to go forward. I gave the order a second time. Still, forward. The third time I jerked her leash and said, "Pfui! Right." This time Topsy went right, and I struck a *No Parking* sign and cut my head. Topsy could have said, "I told you so." That was just after we had left the Seeing Eye. Later, if I insisted that Topsy do what she knew was wrong, she simply sat down and refused to do it.

It is amazing how much Seeing Eye dogs are taught at the school. Yet there are some things they must learn individually. One of the lessons Topsy had to learn was what to do about elevators. She knew how to ride up and down on them. What she did not know was that I had to press the button before boarding the car. At the Biltmore there are three elevators with the bell between the second and third. Topsy quickly learned that if any elevator was standing open we need not press the bell.

During the first day Topsy discovered where the dining room and coffee shop were located. She never ate in the dining room, but I took her little tin bucket there and the chef filled it with food. Sometimes she carried her bucket back to my room. It did not take Topsy long to discover who gave me the food for her and where it might be secured. Anyone who wore a white coat and cap was a friend of Topsy's. She was supposed to eat one meal a day. In the morning, however, I gave her a few dog biscuits; and about five o'clock a serving of meat and vegetables. I have never known Topsy to refuse food, nor do I remember a time when she was completely filled. One morning when the bellboy came to bring the paper he inquired, "How many pieces of toast did you have on your tray?"

"Four," I announced.

"Well, you have two now!" From that day Topsy never had to steal. She merely sniffed at anything I held in my hand, knowing full well that by so doing she would secure it.

When I walked with a friend, I dropped the bar of Topsy's harness, and took her on leash. Then she was not working, for I slipped my hand through the friend's arm. But it was not easy for Topsy to forget her job even when she was not supposed to be on duty. When we came to a curb, she looked to left and right as usual, and if she thought I was not aware of the step, she lifted her head and touched my hand with her nose. She was not taught that gentle reminder by the Seeing Eye.

When Topsy and I began working in Dayton, I was worn out from my rigorous training. Any means of saving energy was seized upon in order to make my new life less difficult. In the center of town there were traffic lights at every intersection. How much easier it would be, I thought, if I crossed with the people. I would not have to bother watching the traffic. It was not long before I discovered that the green light meant very little to the public. Many times I would start with someone, and before I was a quarter of the way across, the individual would jump back to the curb. I soon abandoned this mad practice. I decided, too, that since the streets of Dayton were very wide, I would start at the instant the light turned green. I never tried to cross on a half-spent light, for I disliked standing in the middle of the street while the cars whizzed past. While I was standing on the curb, I did not object to people telling me that the light was green, though I waited until I knew it for myself. When Topsy and I were actually crossing the street, people were not supposed to talk to us. It was dangerous and unfair to the dog. Sometimes when we were crossing and were absorbed in the operation, a well-meaning pedestrian screamed, "Wait!" I jumped, jerked

Topsy's harness, and felt as if I would rather be run down than scared to death.

Topsy never learned to like motorcycles. I think she objected to the noisy putt-putt of the engine. I don't care for them myself, because noise interferes with my faculty of orientation. Perhaps that explains her aversion.

When Topsy began guiding me in Dayton, many people thought she was not careful, and that something surely would happen to me. However, I trusted her, and felt safer with her than with people. No accident has ever been caused through the carelessness of a Seeing Eye dog.

Many street corners have, in recent years, been rounded. This is not so good for blind people, and was certainly a temptation to Topsy, who was always inclined to cut corners. It seemed as if she thought, "What's the use of stepping up on the curb, turning, and stepping down again, when all you have to do is go around." It took Topsy just about once to learn a bad habit. One day when walking with Mrs. Greene, who is always in a hurry, I discovered that she was jaywalking. The next day Topsy did exactly the same thing. It happened so quickly that I was unable to stop her. But when I realized where we were, I corrected her and took her back to the far corner.

"Don't let your dog think he has to go everyplace with you," Mr. Debetaz had said. He might as well have said, "Stop the sun from shining." Topsy certainly did not want to remain at home, and I worried if I left her. What if there were a fire, or someone should steal her? I found all sorts of excuses for taking her with me. The most potent of all was that Topsy herself seemed very wretched over the separation.

During that first summer she chewed the heels off my white shoes three times. The Seeing Eye had warned me that this might happen. Topsy chewed the shoes only in my absence as if she were getting even for being left alone. There was a shutter door to my room with a foot of open space at the bottom. I used this door instead of the regular one most of the time for ventilation. If I left Topsy, which I seldom did, she stuck her head and forefeet under the door and watched for me. If anyone came along and sympathized, she whimpered and acted as if she were in the last stages of desperation.

At the Seeing Eye, the dogs in the kennels are fed at six, turned out in the runs for exercise, and then put to bed for the night. When Topsy came to me, her inclination was early to bed. When I attended lectures or the theatre, Topsy was very good. Perhaps it was because she had a chance to sleep. But if I was not in a place where she must be quiet, and if bedtime rolled by, she crawled into my lap, ran her foot down my treasured nylons, or made a noise in her throat as if she were trying to talk. Sometimes when Topsy wanted her harness off, she would get in front of me as I walked about the room. As soon as I had removed it, she would crawl under the bed.

Topsy loved company as long as they talked about her. When she was ignored, she sighed heavily from time to time as if to say, "Won't they ever go home?"

Where and how comfortably Topsy slept was a vital problem. It never troubled her much, but I gave it considerable thought. In the first place there was no dog bed manufactured large enough for Topsy, and in the second place, if there had been one, there would have been no space left for me in my room. At the Seeing Eye Topsy slept at the foot of my bed. During the day she still followed that practice. At night, however, she crawled underneath. When my room was draughty I tucked blankets around the side and foot of my bed to keep the air from blowing on her. When she got cold in the middle of the night she placed one paw on the side of the bed to waken me and waited until I issued an invitation to jump up. If no invitation was forthcoming, Topsy sighed and crawled dejectedly back to her own bed.

One time I secured a fibra-foam pad. This is the type used in ambulances and I thought it would make a nice bed for her. I had a cover made for it so that it would not smell rubbery. When I put the pad under her bed, Topsy pushed it as far toward the head of the bed as possible, and slept on the floor. These pads sell for ten or fifteen dollars, and though I told her that, it made no difference.

At the Seeing Eye Mr. Debetaz had said, "Never let anyone pet your dog."

"But I don't want a dog people can't pet. It would be difficult to make sixteen hundred children keep hands off." So he modified the statement, "Petting is up to the master."

I decided to let people pet Topsy and if it interfered with her training, I would discontinue the practice. I have never felt that it did interfere. No dog, however, should be petted or talked to while working. As long as I had hold of Topsy's harness, she was apt not to notice my best friend. When crossing the street she never noticed anyone. If, however, we were on the sidewalk, she might take me up to the person and stop directly in front of him. The reward for service was a pat on the shoulder and the exclamation, "Good girl!" Topsy liked to be petted. She not only enjoyed it, she asked for more by poking the person's hand with her nose.

It is curious how people interpret the same behavior in different ways. When Topsy opened her mouth and showed her teeth, catching her lip up under a tooth, the average person thought she was laughing. People who were afraid of her were sure she was snarling. Usually she did this when she was begging, anxious to please, or wanting to attract attention.

Topsy liked children unless they moved so quickly that she was afraid they might hurt me. I think she had never forgotten the little boy who knocked me over the first time she guided me through the streets of Morristown. One day in Rike-Kumler's I tried to leave the elevator, but Topsy seemed to be hanging back. Congressman Jeffrey's little boy had hold of her tail and did not want to let her go.

Daytonians said all sorts of things about Topsy. One woman called her a sight-seeing dog. That she certainly was. Another referred to her as a sight-saving dog. How I wish she had been. But the funniest description was, "Oh, there goes the lady and her blind dog."

In August, Mr. Ebeling and Mr. Humphrey, two executives from the Seeing Eye, came to visit me. Mr. Humphrey tested Topsy and me.

154

"You have made as much progress in two months as you possibly could. Remember, you know more about your dog than anyone in Dayton." His words cheered me, for in a few weeks I was going into school and I did not know how Topsy would behave. During the summer months, I spent much of my time getting Topsy ready. Each day I took her to Steele High School where we walked among hundreds of children and climbed the stairs with the hurrying mob. I took her down the fire escape, for she refused to take me. But I knew that with the opening of school, Topsy and I must descend that steep narrow stairway which led from the third floor down to the second, across part of the roof and onto the ground, in order to bring my students to safety.

August changed to September—summer to fall. Dayton was getting used to Topsy. Topsy and I were becoming as one. Her faithfulness to me was beyond comprehension. My faith in her knew no bounds. But the great problem remained to be solved: Topsy must go to school.

As September began I regarded the opening of school with perturbation. I did not know how Topsy would act. What I did know was that if she did not behave, she could not remain. The first day I worked her through the milling crowd of sixteen hundred high school boys and girls she seemed frightened and a bit confused. I fancied she was afraid, not for herself, but for what might happen to me. We signed the register in the office, I collected my mail, and we hastened upstairs to the third floor. I had given my school procedure considerable thought. Topsy would rest under my desk during class, and could go to the door with me when classes changed. For her comfort, Margaret Sander, one of my students, bought a rag rug and embroidered Topsy's name on it. Topsy was also to go to the auditorium, for she would stay with me constantly. On the first day we made our schedule cards; as a joke we filled out one for Topsy:

NAME:	Topsy Brown. Answers to: Tops, Topper, and Topsy Turvey
BORN:	Dec. 23, 1936, Chicago, Ill.
SCHOOL ATTENDED:	Seeing Eye, Morristown, N. J.
SCHOOL:	Steele High
HOME ROOM:	306
SEAT:	Under desk
CLASSES:	First period. American History
	Second period. American History
	Third period. Lunch and study
	Fourth period. World History
	Fifth period. World History
	Sixth period. American History

Topsy always received "A" in deportment. She never barked in school. Sometimes her tail got stepped on, but she paid no heed.

"I just stepped on Topsy's ear," Madeleine informed me one day.

"Did she do anything?" I questioned.

"Oh, no, ma'am."

"Well, Topsy will have to learn to keep her ear where it belongs. Good girl," I commended. "You know no one really wants to hurt you."

One day Topsy insisted upon walking on the wrong side of the hall. I gave her a jerk and said, "Pfui." She let out a yelp that was heard down on the first floor. I was sure she was trying to get sympathy, for the force of the jerk was not sufficient to merit such a protest.

"What was the matter with Topsy?" Miss Neth questioned, when I saw her later. "I heard her cry and I almost came up to see if she had been hurt."

"She was just playing for sympathy," I explained. "I'm glad you didn't come." That was the only time I can remember when Topsy cried in school.

Sometimes when we stood at the door of my room the students would pet her as they passed. If someone was remiss because he was in a hurry, she poked him with her nose as if to say, "Remember me?" Topsy had many devoted friends among the students and teachers. There was always someone to see that she had fresh water once or twice a day.

She enjoyed most of all the mad rush to the lunch room. We kept pace with the fastest, and if anyone dared to get in our way Topsy pushed him aside with her head. She may have hoped for a bite of meat or candy, and she liked to be in the race. I never made a practice of allowing people to feed Topsy. However, she inveigled many a bite on the sly. Sometimes during the lunch period as we passed through the halls, she would stop and look at a youngster eating a piece of candy. The child usually yielded, and the first thing I knew Topsy was joyously crunching a gum drop.

After school on Tuesday, as sure as death and taxes, we have a faculty meeting. If the session was unusually long, Topsy registered boredom first by a yawn, and then by uttering a small squeak.

I have always tried to maintain a regular time for Topsy's airing. Sometimes this was not possible with a change in schedule. If she felt that she had waited too long, she refused to go back into my room and pulled toward the outside door. When I asked her if she wanted to go out, she wagged her tail joyfully and handed me her paw.

Topsy never disturbed my classes, and I was about to say she never disturbed an assembly. I should say, hardly ever. Once a minister was addressing our student body. Fortunately for me the principal did not seem particularly pleased with the message that was being delivered. Suddenly into the respectful silence came a resounding double sneeze. On the opposite side of the auditorium the assistant principal arose to see what the trouble was. Everybody smiled and looked at me, while Topsy lay at my feet as innocent as a newborn babe.

The passing of classes is controlled by bells. I wondered how Topsy would react to them. At the end of the period there are two bells, one for warning, the other for passing; at the beginning of the new period there is a tardy bell. By the end of the second day Topsy understood the bell system. At the first signal Topsy did not move. Sometimes her nose touched my knee to let me know she was ready, but she never got up. When the passing bell rang, Topsy jumped up as if she had been shot out of a cannon and we hurried to the door to wait in our accustomed place. When the tardy bell rang, I was supposed to re-enter my room. Sometimes a teacher or pupil would detain me for a moment. Then Topsy began to pull at the leash and insisted upon dragging me into the classroom. Apparently she thought I was neglecting my duty.

The firebell is a gong which is struck three times and repeated three times. This bell had a maddening effect on Topsy, and a similar one within me. I had difficulty in restraining her until I saw that the windows were down, the lights off, the children out, and the door closed. Once I decided to let her loose and walk out with one of the students. She went out with the class, but in the confusion lost track of me. She rushed in and out of the building, and was uncontrollable and desperate. It is strange how she sensed that a fire drill might mean real danger.

In the school day I was confident Topsy knew the number of periods before lunch and the number after. If the schedule were changed, however, she became confused and a bit troubled.

Once Topsy served on a roll call for the Red Cross. With a white cap on her head, and a box fastened to the top of her harness, she marched through the school collecting coins from the students. Sometimes, in order to attract attention or to express her disapproval, Topsy would shake furiously so that the lid came off the box and the money flew in all directions. She seemed, though, to enjoy the fun, for she wagged her tail and laughed with her lip caught up by one tooth.

When Topsy first started to Steele, I was constantly cleaning gum from her fur and feet. Finally I discovered that she was filching it from beneath the seats, but a few corrections ended that. Later when she saw a child chewing gum she sniffed, and sometimes her mouth quivered, so the story got abroad that Topsy told me when the students were chewing gum.

When Mr. Painter, our former principal, died, the faculty went to the funeral. Before we started, one of the teachers came to me and said that some of the faculty thought I should not take Topsy. I didn't, but I was wretched, and I felt that they were sorry; never since that time has any teacher made such a request. Since then I have taken Topsy to funerals, and as soon as she entered she sensed the solemnity. If I approached the casket, she hung back just as far as possible.

One day I spoke in an assembly. As I sat down I drew Topsy toward me. At the same instant the curtains came together and there was a burst of laughter. "Topsy's tail was waving gaily outside the curtains," Miss Royal explained.

After Topsy had been at Steele for two years, the Board of Education decided that the school was not safe for the housing of boys and girls. The faculty was transferred to Wilbur Wright High School, and Topsy and I went along.

When I secured Topsy I did not actually need her in school, as I was accustomed to going about the building alone. Wilbur Wright was quite a different proposition, however, for I knew nothing about the location of the offices, classrooms, or lunch-room. Topsy knew all about them the first day.

If the principal sent for me, I would start down the hall and when I came to where I thought the office ought to be, I would say, "Topsy, we're going to go right." But only when she came opposite the entrance would she swing right.

Topsy had her picture taken many times. At first she objected strenuously. Maybe she did not like the flash, or perhaps she knew that pictures seldom did her justice. Her coat was so black that even though she was against a light background it was difficult to catch the sheen of her fur and the expression on her face. Later, when Topsy had her picture taken, she used it as an opportunity to show off. When we were transferred to Wilbur Wright the newsmen came and took pictures of Topsy entering the classroom, under the desk, and sitting at the door. They even went so far as to put her in an empty seat among students; she wore spectacles and sat looking at a book. She seemed to understand that she was putting on an act, and sat blinking her eyes behind the lensless rims.

At Wilbur Wright there is a fifth of a mile track where,

twice a day, a student ran Topsy. Sometimes when the exercise proved too strenuous for the boys, they mounted a bicycle, fastened Topsy to it, and rode round and round. Kenny Bruns, who ran her three years, finally was able to train her to go around the track by herself. Whenever she decided to take a shortcut, Kenny stopped her and made her do it over.

In 1943 after I had been out of school for two and a half months, I let Topsy loose the morning of my return. Joyfully she ran to one student, back to me, then to another. How many times she repeated this greeting, I do not know, but I realized then how much a part of her life the school was, and how beaufully she had learned to adjust herself to the routine, the confusion, and the carefree atmosphere in which she found herself.

CHAPTER TWENTY-TWO

The Years of Freedom

Freedom, when it is newly found, is such a precious thing. When Topsy became my Seeing Eye dog, I felt that I wanted to have new experiences and explore unfamiliar places. I began early to try my wings. I started by visiting friends in Dayton. Sadie lived about a mile and a half south, and though Topsy had been there only in a car, she turned in at the gate without any hesitation. The walk to Marbeth's and back was about five miles. That was a frequent trip, and I soon discovered, by selection, an easier way to go. I only needed to show Topsy where to turn once. The next time, she knew.

The first real testing ground Topsy and I found was the Second Church of Christ-Scientist. We took the bus on the corner opposite the hotel, rode what seemed to be two miles, and walked a square to the church. After that first trip, Topsy knew just where to get off the bus and the exact location of the church. We entered the foyer and ascended the steps to the auditorium. At that time I hadn't the slightest idea how Topsy would behave. We went early in order to get settled. Topsy was as good as she could be. The cordiality of the people toward Topsy was a source of great satisfaction to me, and gave me courage to venture to other places with confidence in her behavior.

One of the reasons I secured a dog was so that she could escort me to movies, to concerts, and to the theatre. Shortly after I brought Topsy home, I decided to try the movies. The picture was *Brother Rat*. The manager of the theatre had told me, "You may take the dog in if she doesn't bark." Topsy has never barked in public. I'm still wondering how the Seeing Eye taught her that. I sat on one side of the theatre at the end of the row. Topsy slept peacefully at my feet. Knitting and listening to the dialogue of the picture, I became so absorbed in the plot that I forgot about her. Suddenly I realized that she was gone.

"Where's Topsy?" I whispered. I had visions of my dog wandering all over that theatre, and both of us being thrown out. It was dark, and Topsy was black.

"Topsy, where are you?" I whispered desperately. Someone turned around in the seat in front of me. It was Topsy. She had climbed up and was looking at the picture! This story was later broadcast by Gil Martin. After *Brother Rat*, Topsy remained on the floor, for I was not sure that the movies were good for her eyes.

My next adventure was the theatre. A friend invited me to see *Mary of Scotland*. We sat in the front row of the balcony with Topsy at our feet. She sat up between the acts for relaxation. Sometime later, I went to buy a ticket to see *The Little Foxes*. Elmer Redelle, the theatre manager, was dubious.

"Tallulah Bankhead would just take my head off," he said, "if Topsy caused a disturbance."

"I brought her to *Mary of Scotland*, and you didn't even know she was there," I informed him. He laughed and relented, and I doubt that Tallulah Bankhead knew Topsy was there either.

One winter the Metropolitan Opera came to Dayton. Josephine Antoine is a friend of mine. I have known her ever since she was in her teens, so naturally I wanted to hear her sing. I bought a seat in the first row where Topsy would have plenty of room to stretch out, not realizing that the orchestra pit would be right in front of us. The musicians were much taken with Topsy, and when they were not playing they were watching or petting her. It was a little too close to the orchestra for me, and probably for Topsy, though she gave no sign, for she never howled when she heard music.

In 1940 I attended the Chicagoland Music Festival luncheon at the Stevens Hotel as the guest of Mrs. Dalmar. I went early and was seated at the table before the crowd came into the dining room. Mrs. McDowell was guest of honor. The chief source of entertainment was the Bengal Drummers. There were seventy-five girls in the group, all of them beating drums with all their might. People sat covering their ears. It might have been all right for out-of-doors, but it was terrible in that dining room. I wondered what Topsy was going to do. I had visions of her howling and bolting from the room, but she never moved. When the concert was over and the luncheon had been served, I coaxed her from under the table so that she could get more air and see the people. I remember the exclamations as she came into view. Poor Topsy had heard that deafening sound and lived!

At the luncheon were the Duncan Sisters, who put on "Topsy and Eva." "Topsy! Topsy!" called Eva. My Topsy was beside herself with excitement. She pulled at the leash and strained to go forward. She wouldn't go without me, yet she was sure she was being called. Afterward, when we met the Duncan Sisters at a tea given by Mrs. Dalmar for the McDowell Society of Evanston, I explained to them how much confusion they had brought to one dog's mind. Eva called "Topsy!" again, and this time Topsy answered by wagging her tail and shaking hands.

Hotels and restaurants are always open to Seeing Eye dogs. The only trouble I ever had was in convincing the people in charge that Topsy *was* a Seeing Eye. Once I was refused entrance by a restaurant owner who wrote me a letter of apology the next day. When we returned to this restaurant, I had an excellent dinner and Topsy was given some steak.

When Topsy had been in Dayton a few weeks, I decided to go to Columbus for the day. Topsy had journeyed from Morristown, but that was in a crate. From now on she would go in the day coach or the Pullman, and her conduct must be above reproach. At the station I bought a ticket and waited for my train. In Dayton, the tracks are built overhead, and as a freight ran above us, Topsy jumped up and strained at the leash as if eager to go aboard. Later we stood beside the tracks and waited for the train from Cincinnati to arrive. I have always hated to have a train pass me. The Seeing Eye had said: "The dog reflects his master." I did not want to give Topsy the fear

I felt. I stood facing the track, steeling my nerves as the engine drew in. This time it was Topsy who tried to turn away. When we were ready to board the train, Topsy did not seem to understand what was expected of her.

"Lady, your dog will have to go in the baggage car," the brakeman said.

"It's a Seeing Eye," I replied, unruffled, as we climbed the steps.

"I beg your pardon, lady," he apologized ."Take her right in."

When we reached Springfield, Topsy thought it was time to get off, but I told her, "No, no," and she rested again. Topsy liked riding on the train; I suppose because she liked riding. Then, too, there were always people to notice and talk to her.

At Columbus I stood up and worked Topsy to the door. She was always eager to get off the train. She acted sometimes as if she thought the train might start with her still on it. I have had exactly the same feeling myself. Often, when we were going down the aisle and people were in front of me, Topsy tried to push them aside with her head. She wanted to be the first one off, and generally was. This first time, however, Topsy was not so brave. She waited to see what other people would do. Finally, we descended to the platform and hurried up the steps, for the tracks at Columbus are under the station.

In the evening, when we returned, Topsy was an old hand.

"Your dog must be used to travelin'," the porter drawled as we stood waiting for the train. "Second trip," I exclaimed. "The first one this morning!" Topsy stood firm as the engine thundered past, head up, tail wagging. As the cars came into view, she began to move toward the steps. She was eager to be aboard, and she didn't want anyone to think that she was unaccustomed to traveling. Her pretense was perfect.

On our return trip I went into the diner, so that Topsy might learn how to work through the cars, and how to behave where there was no table to go under. When I returned to my seat in the coach, the waiter brought a huge hamburger which the steward had sent her. Topsy did not need to learn how to win friends and influence people.

So our first trip ended happily. We may have traveled many thousands of miles since. Usually I tried to make the journey at night unless the day trip was no more than five hours. Topsy never barked or caused any disturbance, but always stayed in her place as a Seeing Eye dog should. In overnight traveling she slept at the foot of my berth, and when the train was not crowded we occupied a small bedroom or drawing room. If the floor became too cold or hard, she climbed stealthily onto my bed, and I awoke to find her curled beside me, sleeping peacefully.

Before and after I secured Topsy, I had done a great deal of lecturing, and with her arrival I added "The Seeing Eye Dog" to my list of topics. She seemed to enjoy these events as much as I did. I'm sure she considered that the lecture was really hers. Usually before I spoke, there was a business meeting or music. Apparently Topsy thought that the applause was always a signal for her to start toward the platform, for she got up, wagged her tail, and pulled in that direction. When we walked onto the stage, the audience applauded. That was the signal for Topsy to show off. Usually the first thing I did was to give her the command, "Down." Topsy disliked this command. I think she felt that she might miss something. When she was sure that I was in a good humor, she put her head on the floor, but kept her hind legs straight. That was her way of bending the rule, not breaking it. On several occasions Topsy assumed this position with her head toward me and her tail wagging at the audience. This seemed to be her way of making a bow. She almost stole the show. During the lecture she remained quietly on the floor at my feet. She looked up at me, or if she found a friendly human down front, she rolled her eyes and laughed. She was usually too interested to sleep.

When I talked to the audience about Topsy, I told them the words she knew. At first this enumeration troubled her no end. Stretched out on the floor at my feet, she couldn't see how she could carry out the commands. I think the thing that disturbed her most was when I said, "Pfui," for she knew she wasn't doing anything wrong. It didn't take her long, however, to get used to hearing these words without obeying them.

Just before the close of my lecture, I put Topsy through her obedience exercises. People always expected me to say something about my dog. When I went to Iowa to speak, someone else was going to lecture on the Seeing Eye, so I ignored Topsy completely. When, however, I attempted to leave the patform, she refused to go. I explained what the trouble was and put her through her obedience of "Come," "Sit," "Down," and "Fetch." Then she trotted joyfully off the platform.

In 1943 I decided to drive with Frances Jones to California, taking the southern route. Topsy stayed in the back of the car, and each day I worried about how she would stand the heat. Each morning, however, she was up and eager to start, though we drove 450 miles a day. We went to El Paso and over the border to Mexico. We stopped at the Carlsbad Caverns and in the evening watched the thousands of bats come out for their soiree. We went through El Centro, where the temperature was 112 degrees, and rested for a short time at San Diego.

When we reached California, I was much the worse for wear, though Topsy ran in the heavy grass and seemed to notice immediately that this was a different world than the one from which she had come. We traveled up the coast and stopped at Oakland for a month's stay. As I was not very well, the doctor suggested that I go back to Chicago as quickly as possible. Strange as it may seem, I was desperately homesick, and time was an important element. By train it would take three days to get back, and I figured that the cost of the trip, including porter and meals, would amount to almost as much as by plane. I could make the trip by air from Oakland to Chicago in fourteen hours, and thanks to Morris Frank and the Seeing Eye, I could take Topsy with me.

I boarded the plane at five-thirty P.M. Topsy climbed up the steps as if she knew all about planes. There may have been a first train ride for Topsy, but there wasn't a first plane ride. With me, it was different. I was afraid, as I so often am, of new things; I was not afraid of accidents, but of flying itself. I noticed that someone locked the door, and that I was strapped loosely into my seat. These precautions did not lessen my anxiety. Topsy seemed completely at home. If she realized that we were not on a train, she must have comforted herself with the thought that it was another ride. Later, someone asked if we were accustomed to flying. I answered that this was my first trip.

"Well, Topsy must be used to it. She climbed into the plane as if she knew all about it."

"She would," I rejoined; "but it's her first trip, too."

Before we started the hostess passed out mammoth sticks of gum. They were supposed to be good for what might ail one. That did not make me feel any easier either. The hostess sat beside me as the plane taxied down the runway. Tears came into my eyes and I found breathing difficult. Topsy lay at my feet, sniffing under the opposite seat to see what she could find.

"We are in the air," the hostess reassured me, and I breathed easier. This was going to be a wonderful trip. I listened to the soft purr of the engines. I could not feel the motion of the plane, except when we hit an air pocket. Then I could feel the drop and the succeeding lift.

We had dinner and breakfast on the plane. I drank my coffee from a cup that fitted into a little slot in the saucer; I dined on rolls that would not disintegrate in the air; my meat had been placed in Thermos containers before we took off, and was ready to serve at dinner time. As there was no table for Topsy to go under, she had a grand time following the hostess about, hoping for a handout, but she fasted until morning. When the hostess had served everyone else, she brought my dinner, and sat down beside me.

"If you'll lean forward, I'll give you a bite of meat," she suggested. Apparently she thought she had to feed me.

We retired early. I wrapped Topsy in a blanket which I had brought for her, and she lay in a straight line beside me and slept like a baby. In Oakland they had told me that the plane would stop at Elko, Nevada, at nine o'clock. When I boarded the plane, I was informed that since we were loaded to capacity we wouldn't stop. Topsy is a good traveler and waited patiently until she was wakened and taken off at Cheyenne at two A.M. for a run.

At eight in the morning, we landed at the Chicago Municipal Airport. The weather had been fine and the trip had been peaceful. Sometimes I have wondered just what Topsy thought about that night flight. Did she know that we were 15,000 feet up, or was it for her just another ride? For me it was a glorious experience, with fear overcome, and the anticipation of more trips by plane in the future.

I have always had a fondness of boat rides. So, whenever I go to Chicago, I take a trip to Milwaukee. Since I could not bear to leave Topsy for the day, I decided to take her with me. The boat left the pier at nine in the morning and we were due to arrive in Milwaukee at three. There was always the question of whether Topsy could survive long trips. She seemed to be at home on the boat, mingling with the people and finding an occasional bite to eat. In Milwaukee I fed her and let her run, and on the boat, once again with my blanket covering her, she slept at my feet until we docked.

Whenever we were near water Topsy's old inclination, swimming, showed up. She leaped and dived and fetched sticks that I threw for her. She refused, however, to go very far out. When she came ashore she shook the water not on me, but on my friends.

In 1940, in order to improve my lecturing, I enrolled in summer school at Northwestern University. My health, however, would not stand the extra effort, so a friend directed me to the office of Dr. Snorf. It developed that Dr. Snorf was from Dayton.

"I don't want to scare you," Dr. Snorf said, "but you should go to the hospital."

"I can't go to the hospital. I can't leave Topsy."

"Topsy can go with you," Dr. Snorf said with assurance. So Topsy and I celebrated the Fourth of July by entering Evanston Hospital. As we went in the porter said, "Dog, too?" But if the nurses were surprised to see Topsy they gave no sign.

Topsy had two worries that day, the fire crackers and the hospital. She lay in the corner, licking her mouth and sighing occasionally. She seemed to know that the nurses were trying to help me. My diet contained no red meat, but chicken and fish twice a day, and I cared little for either. The doctors and nurses were pleased to see my tray come back empty after each meal. Little did they know that it was Topsy who benefited from my diet. In a few weeks I was able to leave the hospital, but not to attend regular classes.

The following summer I re-entered Northwestern, and took a course in prosody under Lew Sarett. Doctor Sarett is a dog lover, and he paid particular attention to Topsy, who always expected it. She remained quiet until time for the bell to ring, when she pricked up her ears in anticipation.

During one class period, Doctor Sarett was trying to demonstrate the effect of a motif in music. He sang the motif. When Topsy could stand it no longer, she jumped up, shook herself, and howled, interrupting the discussion. Everybody laughed, including Doctor Sarett.

"Even the dog can't take it," he said.

In the winter of 1948, I noticed that Topsy was aging, but I, too, was older, so it really did not matter. I spared her whenever I could, but in the spring, Dr. Knapp, who is one of the best surgeons in the country, told me that Topsy had heart trouble and sugar diabetes.

"We aren't going to do anything about the latter," he said, "for I think the shock of insulin shots every day would be too much for her. We'll give her digitalis whenever we feel she needs it, but we can not give it to her constantly, for it is habit forming."

I dreaded the fire drills at school, for I feared she might drop in the midst of things. School closed June eleventh, and on June tenth Topsy and I sat in our accustomed place at Commencement distributing tickets to late-comers. The following Friday I went to see Robert B. French, our new superintendent, in order to secure a month's leave the following year to do some lecturing to see how I liked it, and to earn some extra money. On Monday I went to Columbus to make some lecture contacts, and William Ellis asked me to stay for the Lion's Club meeting on Tuesday.

It was hot, so Topsy and I took a taxi to the Neil House. There were twelve Sight Prevention children there, and they all patted Topsy, and she seemed to be in fine shape. When the luncheon was over, I again took a taxi to the home of friends. The thermometer was climbing, and as we got out of the taxi Topsy began to make a queer squeaking noise in her throat. I gave her the digitalis I was carrying, but she continued her struggling. In the evening I took her to Dr. Knapp before going home.

"I would stay in town tonight," he advised, "and keep her cool and quiet."

But the friends where I had been visiting lived in an upstairs apartment, and each time I took her up those steep steps, I feared she would not make it.

"If I could just get her home," I told Mr. Knapp, "I could take her up on the elevator." I could not think of any place to stay in Columbus. Dr. Knapp suggested that I take an air-conditioned coach home.

Everything went wrong. The train was an hour late; we had to walk almost two blocks to get aboard. Topsy had difficulty getting up the steps, and when I coaxed her onto the seat, it tipped and she fell. I was giving her the medicine as often as I dared. Two people from Dayton fanned her all the way home. We took her down into the station in the elevator and out into the taxi, and all the way she kept trying to lie down.

The next morning I phoned Dr. Oldham. He said there was nothing he could do and that she would be worse off away from me. So I sat and watched her struggle. About five o'clock in the evening, I went for a sandwich. When I came back, Topsy was at the door awaiting my return. At 6:30 she came over to me and put her head in my lap. I thought she wanted me to help her, but perhaps she was trying to tell me what I could not realize. I called Mr. Helwagen, an ardent admirer of Topsy, and asked him to bring over another fan. Then I noticed she had stopped struggling, and I thought she was asleep. When Mr. Helwagen had connected the fan, he knelt down beside her.

"She's breathing easier," he said, as Topsy laid her head on his arm. "She's breathing too easy," he continued. "She's gone."

I could not believe him, though I knew he was telling the

170

truth, so I sent for Dr. Claggett who lives at the Biltmore. He didn't even go over to her; he merely looked at her and verified the statement of Mr. Helwagen. Topsy died when she was exactly eleven and a half years old.

While the newspapers and radio stations were telling Daytonians that the first Seeing Eye dog in Dayton had died, we buried her in the dog cemetery beneath the shade of two large trees and within hearing distance of the kennels. A friend read this bit of verse as we laid her to rest:

> Father in Thy starry tent
> I kneel, an humble suppliant.
> A dog has died this day on earth,
> Very dear and of great worth.
> Gather her within Thine arms,
> If only for a little while.
> I fear she will be lonely, God,
> Please shield her with Thy smile.

And now I was alone.

Since I had planned to go to Northwestern to work on my book that summer, I left Dayton the following day. Outside my window at the university stretched the lawns where Topsy had rolled and run and turned somersaults. There, too, were some of the friends she had known and loved. I hoped there would be another dog, but there could never be another Topsy. We had ten glorious years together. They meant freedom for me, but restraint for her, though I am sure she loved every minute of that restraint. I still had my writing and lecturing to urge me forward, and who could say what new dreams might lay beyond the horizon to keep me occupied until I join Topsy in eternity?

CHAPTER TWENTY-THREE

Personality Plus

I knew as soon as they carried Topsy's body from my room, that I could not get along without a dog, so within the hour I was calling the Seeing Eye. However, I felt I must get away, so I left for Northwestern the following day. My friends at Evanston listened patiently to the story of my loss until gradually I talked less and less about it, though the utter loneliness still remained. Both my heart and my hands seemed empty. I needed some new undertaking to absorb my interest, so, with a white cane, I began going about the streets of Evanston just as Topsy and I had done in the past. She had taught me the paths to follow and though she was no longer with me, she was always in my mind. No one objected to my venture. They seemed to understand that peace could come only through challenge.

The Seeing Eye wrote that they did not have a retriever small enough for me to handle so they would have to find one. I felt I must have a retriever since Topsy had been so satisfactory for my needs in school. Masters of guide dogs are loath to change breeds, for strange as it may seem, they consider their dog superior to all others.

Early in August, the Seeing Eye wrote that they had found a black Labrador retriever for me and I was to come for training the middle of September. When I wrote to ask what my new dog's name was, they said they could not give me any further information. I taught for a week when school opened, and then, once more, I left for the Seeing Eye.

During the ten years since my last visit many changes had been made. Mr. Debetaz was now head of the school and two classes were being trained simultaneously. There were six-

teen dogs instead of eight and a new wing had been added to the
main building to accommodate the additional students. The procedure was the same, however, only this time I roomed with a
girl from Florida, and my trainer was Mr. Lee.

I waited in eager anticipation for my dog. Finally I sat once
more in the living room with a piece of meat in my hand while
my dog was led in to me. But this dog needed no coaxing to take
my introductory tidbit and trotted with me, gaily wagging, to
my room. Her name, Mr. Lee had said, was Miss Effie, which
became Effie for short. I must confess, I was a little disappointed
when I heard it. I could easily have changed it to something like
Ebony but I know now that she could never have lived up to
such a dignified name. Only "Effie" would fit.

My roommate frequently played with her dog, Lucky, but
my relationship with Effie was quietly restrained. I told Mr. Lee
that I was teaching her to behave in school, but the truth was that
I resented her because of the loss of Topsy. "A second dog is like
a second husband," they told us, "you love each in a different
way."

It was going to take more than this advice to bring me to
my senses. I was still living in the past.

There were eight members in our class, three girls and five
boys. Five of us were there for our second dog. The classes were
never allowed to mingle because the dogs in each class knew
only their own classmates. We occupied separate quarters, sat
at different tables in the dining room, and rode in separate station
wagons on our frequent trips to Morristown. For the first few
days, our class sat at one long table for our meals, then the long
table was replaced with smaller tables which seated two students
each. I was placed with a young band leader from Missouri who
was nervous and ill at ease. I recalled the misery of my first training period and tried to help the boy adjust.

In our class there was also a Negro, Mr. Smith, who was sixty
years old. He had been blind for seven years and had never gone
any place alone. He always wanted to train with me; I suppose
it was because we were nearly the same age. As we got into the
station wagon, he would exclaim, "I wants to walk with Doc

Brown." Sometimes Mr. Lee would let him, but not always because it is better for dog and master to change partners.

We worked in pairs. Mr. Lee went over the route with us and then we were expected to do it without him. One of the routes was called Three-Two-One. This meant three squares south, two squares east, and one square north and since the streets were so crooked, this brought us back to where we had started. On our first trip alone Mr. Smith and I were chosen to walk together. The person in the lead waited at the corner for the other before crossing the street.

"Doc Brown," Mr. Smith would call at every corner as I stood waiting, "is you thar?"

I urged him on until we finally completed the route, returning to the station wagon, and I heard Mr. Lee exclaim, "Here we are." Mr. Smith's joy knew no bounds and I shall never forget how he laughed and cried over his first trip alone since his blindness.

The training was not so severe as the first time and in seventeen days I was back in Dayton. There were the usual interviews and photographs for the papers and then Effie and I went to school and presented ourselves to the faculty and to the students. Mr. Holmes, my principal, took Effie around to every classroom in the building. Poor, little, scared Effie; it hurts me to think of it now. In the course of a few months, Effie had been taken from her home, wherever that was, operated on, trained at the Seeing Eye, given another master, brought to Dayton on a train, and introduced to a school of 1,400 vivaciously adoring boys and girls. Added to this, while I did not neglect or mistreat her, I did not at first give her the love and affection she deserved.

In January, Effie became seriously ill. One of my friends, Bud Rollman, had taken her for a walk and when they came back she lay on the rug shivering. When we took her to the veterinary, her temperature was 104.9 degrees and the doctor did not know whether he could save her. Then I realized how much Effie meant to me and as I nursed her back to health, I tried to win her affection. I bought a large comfortable chair for her to sleep in and in the spring I had her tonsils removed. I was taking no further chances with my best-loved friend.

Effie's coat is short and satiny and she weighs about sixty pounds—forty pounds less than Topsy weighed. Her ears are long and silky, her eyes are brown, and unlike most dogs, her gaze is steady. Her I.Q. is higher than Topsy's and she is unusually friendly. If Topsy was a saint, Effie is certainly an imp and many are the stories of her escapades.

When Effie first came to the hotel, she hated elevators. She scurried on and off them as if she were thinking, "If I *have* to go through this ordeal, I may as well get it over with as soon as possible." Now she has learned to board the elevator herself, ride down to the first floor, go out for her airing, wait for the elevator, and return to the sixteenth floor. She has never gotten off at the wrong floor.

I believe Effie has the most fun at school. One day in the fall, I sent one of my students to the office. Effie wanted to go along and I suggested that he take her for I knew the exercise would be good for her. When he returned, I did not notice that Effie was not with him. By the end of the period Effie still had not returned. I went to the principal's office and told him Effie was missing. "Oh, well," he said without concern, "she'll come back."

I was worried so I went to the assistant principal and told him. He evinced the same unconcern. Nancy, my reader, and I went outside to try to find her. My heart was pounding and I was sick with dread. Effie did come back all right, dragging a telephone lineman behind her. He had been bringing her back to school when she saw me, whereupon she brought him.

One morning a representative from Northwestern University called on Mr. Holmes. He flung his hat on a chair in the outer office and went inside. Effie found the hat and almost made mincemeat of it before we could rescue it. It was bent and wet and no doubt soiled. Mrs. Wagner, the secretary, straightened it out as well as she could and I waited anxiously for the man to reappear. Suddenly he rushed out of the inner office, grabbed his hat without looking at it, and left hurriedly—much to my relief.

Then there was the day that I was assigned hall duty. The

school is built in the shape of a rectangle with stairways at the four corners. It was my job to keep the students in the lower hall during the lunch hour so I walked around and around the halls checking each stairway. At first Effie accompanied me willingly, but as time passed, she could see no sense in this trek, so she sat down and I continued alone. As soon as I got out of sight she ran to catch up with me and sat down again. This went on all during the lunch period and the teachers called it Effie's sit-down strike.

Christmas was a gala time for Effie. Someone was always kept busy tying bells on her collar because she chewed them off as fast as they were put on. One Christmas the class decided to have a party. The refreshments were chocolate covered ice cream bars and when I said that Effie was not allowed to eat the chocolate, the students patiently pealed it off and fed her the ice cream.

Once I was on a T.V. panel to collect money for the Red Cross. Effie had quite a time. She sat on the chair beside me, put her feet in the dish containing the contributions, and stuck her nose in the camera.

One morning when Effie was out by herself for her airing, she started down the alley toward the Elks Club. The doorman at the hotel went after her. She turned and grinned at him and gaily scampered out of reach. The more he chased, the farther she scampered. He was frantic when he called me, but I assured him she would come back. I had learned that if I wanted her it was unwise to give chase. I merely had to walk in the other direction and ignore her and she would come bounding to my side. Though I have never left her, Effie seems to be afraid that she will lose me. She loves a good run but she loves me more.

Effie adores automobiles. She shows a marked preference for my friends who have cars. When we go for a ride, she sits proudly on the back seat and never seems to grow tired of the wind on her face. But trains are a different story. She begins to cry if we even go in the direction of the station. Once on board the train she refuses to sit on the seat or rest on the floor but insists on standing in the aisle where the conductor and brakemen must pet her when they pass. In the beginning I believe she was really afraid but now I think it is an act to get attention. When I take a small bedroom, however, she pants continuously until I am afraid she will go into convulsions. I have sometimes wondered if she suffers from claustrophobia.

Besides her service to me, Effie's life will be remembered as a series of funny episodes. Laughing at these experiences has kept me from growing old.

When I was sixty-five, I decided to retire from teaching because I wanted more time for rest and other interests. Effie likes to sleep late but I am sure that when I am not teaching she misses the students. I'm glad I do not know how much longer Effie and I will go on together, but I hope it will be quite a few years.

A few years ago Effie became quite lame. The doctors say she has arthritis. We give her cortisone for relief but though she may be in pain, she still has the same zest for life, the same love of adventure, and the same devotion to me.

CHAPTER TWENTY-FOUR

Progress Through Change

In 1940, out of a clear sky, Steele High School was declared unsafe for high school boys and girls and abandoned. I was in Evanston hospital for anemia at the time and the news came as a complete surprise. My anemia together with the impending transfer to Wilbur Wright High School seemed almost insurmountable, but I realized that teaching was my bread and butter and I tried hard to make the adjustment.

In Dayton, opposition to the move was strong. In order to keep the memory of Steele alive, an alumni association of 1100 members was organized. There was in their hearts, I suppose, the hope that one day there might be another Steele. I recall with warmth the first meeting of the Association when I was made an honorary member. Over the years the membership of the Alumni has dwindled until now Steele lives only in memory.

On my sixty-seventh birthday the Steele Alumni and the Montgomery County Association for the Blind gave me a birthday party in the Italian Cloister and gardens of the Dayton Art Institute. It was a beautiful evening for a party. Swans bathed in the fountains while more than four hundred friends and former students of mine extended their congratulations and best wishes.

There were speeches by the Superintendent of Schools, Mr. French, and my principal, Mr. Holmes, and some of my former students, among them ex-Congressman Harry Jeffrey. The colors of the two schools, Steele and Wilbur Wright, were represented in flowers.

There was a huge birthday cake furnished by the Rike-Kumler Company and decorated with pastel fruits and flowers worked in the icing. The climax of the evening came with the opening of the gifts. The two organizations presented me with a typewriter and there were many other gifts from friends which the Sightless Children of Dayton helped me to open.

The Association for the Blind prepared a birthday booklet about me which included pictures of Effie and Topsy, and some of my poems and treasured letters.

After Steele was abandoned, the old building was occupied for fourteen years by the Board of Education, the Red Cross, and the Army, intermittently. In the summer of 1953, the site was sold to The Rike-Kumler Company for a parking lot. For months I was forced to breathe the dust and listen to the din as the once familiar halls and classrooms of old Steele were beaten down by the destructive machines of progress. Again and again I reminded myself that "we progress through change," as another former student, Robert Oelman, now president of the National Cash Register Company, says. But the lawns where Effie and Topsy played and the building where I spent so many happy hours are no more.

> But if there's a Heaven for buildings
> With records noble and fair,
> I shall travel the streets till I find it
> For I know that old Steele will be there.

Everything around me is changing and sometimes it seems that I alone am standing still, yet I know that for me there can be no periods of inaction. In order to be happy I must go on to "fresh fields and pastures new."

The move to Wilbur Wright High School in 1940 was not as difficult as I had anticipated, though I began teaching American History for the first time. This shift was indeed a broadening of my field of knowledge for which I have always been grateful. One of the outstanding changes was a freshman home room which proved a real joy and in the years that have passed it has seemed to me that I have handled more freshmen than other classmen and somehow I have grown to like it.

If I have failed to mention many students from Wilbur

179

Wright High School it is because they are still maturing and trying to find their places in local activities. One boy, however, stands out in my mind and in business—Vic Cassano. Only the other day Vic said to me, "I would do 'most anything for Dr. Brown. She taught me to think. I owe my success to her." And as the "King of Pizza" in Dayton, he is truly a success. Surely I am getting my reward from the stories and sayings of my boys and girls, not in heaven but right here in Dayton, Ohio.

Wilbur Wright, however, presented the problem of transportation in that the doctor said I could not wait for buses. To my rescue came Mildred Purviance, a former student and dean of girls, and others. It is surprising how problems solve themselves with friends and time. I never hesitate to ask my former students to assist me and as many are now teaching, I can turn to them for favors. The years at Wilbur Wright were happy ones though as I grew older I found myself worrying about the students that would not study and other things, so in 1953 I retired. I wanted to be free to do some of the things I had dreamed of. I wanted to live longer but strange as it may seem, I began substituting in the fall. The laws of Ohio allow a retired teacher to substitute fifty-nine days each year, so the love of my profession together with financial pressure and the desire to maintain the same standard of living have kept me at Wilbur Wright.

Substituting is a real challenge! I must handle hundreds of students I have never seen before and teach subjects I have long since forgotten, such as Algebra, Geometry, General Mathematics, General Science, Dramatics, Typing, and Journalism. Sometimes the teacher's schedule calls for large study halls. I think the largest I have controlled is one hundred forty freshmen crowded into the school cafeteria but with the co-operation of Mr. Herrman, the assistant principal, it does not take long for me to reach my students and for them to discover that I am conscious of their behavior at all times. Sometimes when I grow especially tired I wish that I could end my teaching but last year when I was experiencing such a feeling, a freshman came to me after class and said, "I am so glad I have had you as a teacher, you are the best teacher I have ever had." It gave me a real lift and made me

180

know that my work as a teacher is not yet finished and I forgot for the time that I was tired.

Just the other day I was shown a composition by a student, Catherine Conner, on the subject "The Most Outstanding Teacher":

> There is a teacher at Wilbur Wright High School. She is a substitute. Dr. Brown is blind. She has a black dog named Effie who leads her around. Dr. Brown substitutes for just about anything. She substitutes for Science, English, Art, and others. She can tell if somebody is talking, or walking around the room. And if she gives you an assignment you better do it. She is very smart. She gets along with us very well.

If anyone believes that retirement is inactivity for me they are wrong. During my spare time, I read, knit, sell cards and stationery, give lectures, travel, and study. Every summer I attend Northwestern University, the brightest spot in my existence. I love every minute of it and I begin planning for my return as soon as the session is over. This summer I studied the Psychology of Personality but most of the time I enroll in interpretative reading under Charlotte Lee or take a course in Political Science under Dr. McGovern. Northwestern and Willard Hall are a real tonic as they afford me association with wonderful people and friends who are as interested in the joy of living as I.

Three years ago I took a brief trip to New York where I saw a play and visited C.B.S. Television whose president, Frank Stanton, is a former student. Sometimes I grow homesick for New York and Columbia and I know I shall return.

Since I am not teaching every day, I joined the Montgomery County Association for the Blind, in order to do whatever I can to help my people. Most of my life has been spent with the sighted but I have always been interested in the blind and I find myself wishing that they might have employment, better homes, and a higher standard of living. Blindness is enough of a cross without poverty and most of my people have little. This year I became president of the Montgomery County Association for the Blind and it is my desire to further their aims as much as possible.

As this manuscript goes to press, Effie is eleven and a half years old and I am seventy-one. Effie is a little old and stiff but her efficiency and her devotion have not lessened. As for myself, I rest a little more and do a great deal of thinking. Occasionally I find myself wondering why, when I gave my best to the State of Ohio, I receive less pension than teachers who retired after nineteen fifty-five. For those who do not know, Ohio ranks seventh in private wealth and this inadequacy is a blot on the state's escutcheon. Perhaps if all the teachers in active service and those who have retired since fifty-five would band together and demand that this inequality be removed, this condition might be remedied.

Such broodings are not of long standing, however. I love life! I try to live it to the fullest. I know that my needs will be met, they always have been. For God walks beside me and guides my halting feet.

CHAPTER TWENTY-FIVE

How to Make Dreams Come True

Years ago I began to think of my successes and to analyze the procedure I had followed in order to bring them about. There was a long road ahead of me; there were many things I hoped to accomplish.

There are some things we accept without questioning. So it is that I have from the beginning believed in a Divine Power, God, who is concerned with my success and failure, my trials and heartaches, and my prayers and problems. Of course, I may put certain limitations on Him, according to my beliefs, and by so doing make Him my particular concept. But God is still God, and ready to help when I call upon Him.

I do not believe in a god who punishes; neither do I believe in a Being who restricts my actions, but One who allows to me the freedom of choice. God, to me, is a loving protector and guide to whom I may turn whenever I desire, to whom I may raise my eyes and find courage, and to whom I may pray and receive an answer.

Recently I have read a number of books whose authors say they do not believe in God. This is hard for me to comprehend, and it grieves me that they must struggle on without having the Divine Source from which to draw strength. I do not know of any handicapped person who does not believe in God, and I am wondering if there are any. I am sure that if I want to live at peace with myself, I must keep my belief in the Almighty.

But you ask, "How do I know there is a God?" and I answer, "By my faith, which 'is the evidence of things not seen.'" I have known at times the deepest kind of loneliness, loneliness which seemed almost impossible to endure, and then, suddenly, without any explanation, I feel that I am no longer alone. There is a presence with me.

I liked to read the stories of our boys at the front, who prayed in their extremity and saw miracles performed, and knew that God was with them. I'm thinking of such experiences as J. D. Whitaker's "We Thought We Heard the Angels Sing." There have been many occasions when I have found faith and strength to carry on beyond my own endurance. That faith and strength can come only from a power that is greater than I. My faith in God has brought me fullness of life, spiritual companionship, and hope. I may question, and the answer may not always come, but I know that whatever I make of my life rests primarily with me.

In order to work out a life philosophy, I have read many books, and attended many churches. Out of my questioning and reasoning came the belief that within reason I could accomplish whatever I wished. But I soon discovered that I must work with singleness of purpose and center my energies on the object of my desire. I must live and breathe and dream it. I must sacrifice for it, and, above all, I must have faith that it will materialize.

When I went to college, it was that way. When I wanted a job, nothing else was quite so important. What, then, were the means I had used? During my first years of teaching, as I looked back on my college days and my first job, I tried to formulate the rules which had governed me during those days when everyone had doubted and I alone had kept faith.

The first rule, I decided, was that I must be true to myself. I must do the best job possible, and not allow my handicap to stand in my way. I, more than anyone else, knew my true self. I must live up to that self, and not to what people expected of me. Because of my blindness, people expected less from me than I knew I could give.

For my second rule, I chose the cultivation of the best in life: the best books, the best poetry, the most inspirational music, and people who possessed the strength and courage I needed. In the crises of life, I knew that anything less would not suffice. I recalled that in stress I had repeated the Twenty-third Psalm or "Pippa Passes." In good books I had found experiences I had not known. I had lived with their heroes, had suffered and found joy with them until they became almost a part of my own life. I had gained strength from Milton, had learned of love from Elizabeth Barrett Browning, and had cried with David Copperfield, and all these experiences had lifted me and given me strength and vision. I recalled the people who had had a great deal to do with my success. I could not even estimate how much they had done for me, how much I had been changed through knowing them.

The third rule, I decided, was to think. Nicholas Murray Butler once said: "Five per cent of the people think, five per cent think they think, and ninety per cent do not think at all." I would strive to be in the first five per cent. I knew I was not brilliant, but so long as I could think clearly I would know pretty much where I was going and why.

Fourth, I would work. I discovered that few people know how to work; and that most people spend more time trying to get out of work than they do in actual labor. A maid once told me, "I want my rooms full. I likes people so I likes to work." When I have a goal for which I am striving it is easy to work. It is hard not to.

Last, and of most importance, I must pray. I must pray believing that I shall receive. There is, however, another kind of prayer which I am sure is more necessary to our spiritual growth, and which for the most part, we are prone to forget. It is the prayer of thanksgiving which should come both before we make a request of God and after. Thankfulness is as necessary to our progress as water and sunshine to flowers, and yet in our joy we overlook it. If you try giving thanks instead of asking you will be surprised to find how many problems work themselves out without effort.

These, then, were the five rules I had used. Be true to yourself, cultivate the best in life, think, work, and pray. These precepts I still use, and if I do not make a success of an undertaking it is because I have not kept my desire single or I am not hitting on all five.

In searching for what I believed and how I wanted to live

I came upon "My Creed" by Howard Arnold Walter. It furnishes the standard by which I strive to live: "I would look up and laugh, and love, and lift." After I had worked out "How to Make Dreams Come True" I began to put my theory into practice, for I felt certain then, and I know now, that it will work. I wanted to share this insight with others. I gave lectures on the subject to high school groups, teachers, and clubs. I wanted them to experience the joy I felt in my new-found freedom, that their dreams too, might be realized.

And ever I strive to set for myself two tasks: I must be able to make adjustments, and I must have vision.

> Smilingly, out of my pain,
> I have woven a little song;
> You may take it away with you.
> I shall not sing it again.

—Aline (Mrs. Joyce) Kilmer